MARTA

CHARLOTTE BROWNE

ULTIMATE
FOOTBALL HEROES

MARTA

FROM THE PLAYGROUND
TO THE PITCH

DINO

Published by Dino Books,
an imprint of John Blake Publishing,
The Plaza,
535 Kings Road,
Chelsea Harbour,
London SW10 0SZ

www.johnblakebooks.com

www.facebook.com/johnblakebooks
twitter.com/jblakebooks

First published in paperback in 2019

ISBN: 978 1 78946 107 7

British Library Cataloguing-in-Publication Data:

A catalogue record for this book is available from the British Library.

Design by www.envydesign.co.uk

Printed and bound in Great Britain by Clays Ltd, Elcograf S.p.A.

1 3 5 7 9 10 8 6 4 2

John Blake Publishing is an imprint of Bonnier Books UK
www.bonnierbooks.co.uk

To my older brother Richard,
for his helpful Portuguese translations

ULTIMATE
FOOTBALL HEROES

Charlotte Browne knew from a young age she would probably
end up working with words. She has worked as a journalist for a
number of publications, from *The Independent* to *Prima*, and written
for organisations within the not-for-profit and charity sectors.
She is probably at her happiest walking in the Cornish countryside,
swimming in the sea or playing her favourite songs on piano.
She lives in south London.

Cover illustration by Dan Leydon.
To learn more about Dan visit danleydon.com
To purchase his artwork visit etsy.com/shop/footynews
Or just follow him on Twitter @danleydon

CONTENTS

CHAPTER 1 – **PRAYING FOR RAIN** 9

CHAPTER 2 – **TINY BUT TOUGH** 14

CHAPTER 3 – **DAYDREAMS AND AMBITIONS** 19

CHAPTER 4 – **THE RIVERBED** 24

CHAPTER 5 – **JUST ONE MINUTE** 30

CHAPTER 6 – **BETTER THAN THE BOYS** 39

CHAPTER 7 – **OPPORTUNITY KNOCKS** 44

CHAPTER 8 – **'BUT SHE'S A GIRL!'** 51

CHAPTER 9 – **NEW BOOTS AND HOME BATTLES** 57

CHAPTER 10 – **UNION AND STRENGTH** 63

CHAPTER 11 – **BACK ON THE MARKET** 71

CHAPTER 12 – **HEADING FOR RIO** 76

CHAPTER 13 – **THE BIG CITY** 84

CHAPTER 14 – **'THE POWER IN THAT LEFT FOOT!'** 89

CHAPTER 15 – **NATIONAL TEAM** 97

CHAPTER 16 – **THE WORLD CUP** 105

CHAPTER 17 – **THE MOVE TO SWEDEN** 112

CHAPTER 18 – **UMEA TRIUMPHS** 118

CHAPTER 19 – **MEDALS AND AWARDS** 124

CHAPTER 20 – **THE QUEEN OF FOOTBALL** 130

CHAPTER 21 – **CHINA 2007** 135

CHAPTER 22 – **LIVING IN AMERICA** 141

CHAPTER 23 – **CALIFORNIA DREAMING** 147

CHAPTER 24 – **'FORÇA BRASIL!'** 153

CHAPTER 25 – **PRIDE** 160

CHAPTER 1

PRAYING FOR RAIN

Alagoas, Brazil. 1987.

In the shade of their house's veranda, Dona Tereza sheltered from the intense heat of the Brazilian midday sun. She watched her sons José and Valdir playing on the streets outside. They'd just come back from church and were eager to stretch their legs, in spite of the heat.

Tereza took hold of the hand of her one-year-old daughter Marta, who had been learning to walk,

and helped her take tiny steps up and down the porch. In such hot conditions, Tereza longed to take a break before her long shift at the plantation started, a job where she had to treat and plant crops in the hard soil.

Her neighbour Emelia walked up the steps and fanned herself with a church leaflet. 'Oh, when will the rain come?' Emelia sighed.

After another long hot summer, the whole neighbourhood was praying for rain, just a little rain to make the crops grow. As Tereza and Emelia looked out at the sun-scorched and cracked brown earth, they longed for something green to appear. Even the cactuses that lined the roadside were turning brown.

'Oh, when the time's right,' replied Tereza. And when that rain arrived, they'd be out there collecting as much water as they could in buckets, to help their own crops grow in the neighbourhood.

Tereza chuckled a little when she considered what a contradiction the name of their home city was. Dois Riachos translated as 'two little rivers'. Even more of a contradiction was the name of the coastal state: Alagoas, named after its enormous lakes. She sighed as she dreamt of magically transporting the children to the cool of Lagoa Manguaba (the

Manguaba Lagoon) or Lagoa do Sul (the Lake of the South). But those places were at least three hours away by bus – or car if you could afford that luxury.

She smiled as she thought of days long ago. She remembered a once-in-a-lifetime childhood trip to the coast at Maceió, the state capital of Alagoas. It was a beautiful stretch of coastline, lined with palm trees and white sands, and she had dipped her feet in the sea. Not quite Ipanema Beach but close enough – years later, she could still recall the sounds of samba music filtering out from a radio from one of the bars.

It was all a world away from Dois Riachos, where she lived now, a town known only for its dry climate, cane-cutting industry and hazardous potholes that lined the roads. They were surrounded by the sertão – the 'wilderness'.

Tereza often felt they may as well be wandering alone in the back waters, as though the entire country had forgotten they even existed.

And now it seemed as though the water – the relief of rain – had forgotten them too.

She looked out to her children and her spirits

lifted when she saw how carefree they looked.
They were playing in the debris of yet another dust
devil, a type of mini-whirlwind that shot up coke
cans and crisp packets from overflowing bins – not
uncommon when the ground heated up to excessive
temperatures. But even the prospect of scorching
their feet didn't stop them from running and playing.
They were too excited.

Down by a dried-up riverbed, they'd discovered a
deflated and disused football that they couldn't wait
to kick around. Other kids from the neighbourhood
soon joined them, whooping with delight at their
new find, and a high-spirited game was soon in full
swing as they picked up cans from the storm for a
makeshift goal.

Tereza felt happy to see her children having fun
and concentrating on play. Since their father Aldário
had left, times had been particularly hard and it was
difficult to even find the money for food. He was
not the only man to leave a family behind. When
there was no food to harvest there was little work
to go round, in a town that depended so much on

agriculture. Aldário was a barber by trade, but people barely had the money to feed their families, let alone keep their beards trim.

In the absence of her husband, Tereza relied on her eldest son José, who was now eleven years old, and a community of close friends and relatives to look after her four children. Some days she left at 5am to work on the plantation and even after her shift finished, she had a second job at city hall, where she'd clean and serve coffee.

As with many of the other mothers in the street, she felt sad she couldn't afford to buy her children a new football but she smiled again, marvelling at their ingenuity. Nothing could stop them playing their favourite game, a game so instinctively pure and simple, yet one so woven into their culture.

CHAPTER 2

TINY BUT TOUGH

The previous year, 1986, the year Marta was born, Brazil had reached the World Cup quarter finals, and half the community had crowded into Romero's Bar, in the town square, to watch the team's progress on a small TV screen. José and Valdir had been there, watching spellbound as their favourite players glided and pirouetted through the air, performing the 'futebol arte' (art-football) that the Brazilian team was so famed for.

And now, one year on, here they were, dancing their way through the heat, dust and debris, re-enacting and practising those moves in the heat of the day. The old football they had just found had long perished and lost any of its former bounce, but Tereza knew it would be one of their most prized possessions. They all played on with it relentlessly, as though their lives depended on it, and she looked on in wonder at the 'fome de bola' (ball hunger) that every Brazilian boy seemed to be born with.

As Tereza watched, she quietly prayed. Was she in the presence of the next Pelé or Garrincha, she thought hopefully? What were the other options for them here anyway? It might be their best bet to get out of this place. She sent them to the local primary school and taught them what she could at home but they couldn't afford new books. Alagoas had the lowest literacy rate of any of Brazil's twenty-six states and some of Tereza's friends struggled to read or write at all. She knew they had little future unless the town became more industrial and had better jobs.

Emelia spoke, as if she were able to hear Tereza's prayer.

'They could be, Tereza, they could be... If the rains won't rescue them... maybe football will!'

Emelia had a point. Hadn't Pelé grown up in the poorest part of São Paulo?

'The poorest part of the *favelas*,' she explained, using the Brazilian word for 'slums'. 'He played football with a sock stuffed with newspaper!'

'Don't let my sons know,' said Tereza. 'We need our laundry!'

'I have to stop my two from stealing the grapefruit. We need to eat them – not kick them! *Minha nossa!*' They both laughed.

'At least you also have two girls to balance it out!' said Emelia.

Tereza nodded and looked over at her daughter Angela, who was singing to her dolly and rocking it back and forth in her hands. Suddenly, she realised she didn't still have Marta's hands gripped in hers.

'Oh look!' gasped Emelia.

Marta was toddling out into the street towards where the children were playing. Tereza had tried to put her in a dress for church but she'd wrestled out of it. She preferred her brother's hand-me-down T-shirt, which was far too big for her.

Barefoot, Marta was a little shaky on her feet and kept looking as though she was about to topple but she doggedly carried on. Her brothers took little notice of her, lost in their game. They only spotted her when José lost control of the ball and inadvertently kicked a load of dust in her face as it rolled towards her. Marta didn't seem to notice – her attention was fixed on the ball.

'Marta!' Tereza called, and then shouted, 'Careful, boys!'

She ran towards Marta, exclaiming, 'Her feet must be scorching!'

As she got closer, Tereza noticed the stubborn expression on Marta's face. She was tiny, even for her age – Valdir called her '*pequeña*' – but she could really stand her ground.

'Ha ha!' Her brothers laughed at her. 'The ball's almost the same size as her!'

Marta stared back at them, her dark brown eyes glaring.

'Go on then... go on – kick it back!'

Marta kept staring at them, hunched her chin and

shoulders down – and, to her mother's amazement, took some backward steps.

Valdir moved towards her to pick the ball up but before he could, Marta kicked it towards him. He cried out in surprise as it hit his shin. José burst out laughing at his younger brother.

'Valdir – you chicken!'

An expression of sheer joy crept over Marta's face that Tereza hadn't seen before. She protested as her mother picked her up and carried her back inside.

'Wow! *Minha nossa!*' cried Emelia. 'Indeed, she may be tiny but she's tough!'

CHAPTER 3

DAYDREAMS AND AMBITIONS

'And what do you want to be when you grow up, Marta?' Her teacher gazed down at her disapprovingly, as though already anticipating an unconventional answer.

'A footballer, Miss.'

The class sniggered.

'But Marta, you're a girl.'

Marta sighed. This was a phrase she'd heard for as long as she could remember. Since the age of five when she'd first asked her mum for money (one real) to buy a football. Since her mum told her off for scuffing her clothes when she was practising bicycle kicks, 'just like Rivaldo, Mum!' Since she'd had to be

dragged away, kicking and screaming, for watching
Mexico '86 reruns on video all night when she
should have been in bed.

The teacher looked down at the scrawlings on the
girl's notepad.

'What are you drawing, Marta?'

'Rivaldo, miss.'

'She wants to be just like him when she grows
up,' laughed one girl. It was true – Rivaldo played
exactly as Marta wanted to play. She would watch
the boys play in the same way: attack, attack, attack
– always getting in there, looking for chances.

'Macho man!' cackled another girl.

'Marta, Marta...' sighed her teacher. 'Answer me
when you have a different answer, okay? Otherwise
you're wasting my time.'

'A different answer?'

'A normal answer, Marta.'

'But she's not normal, Miss,' said a boy sitting
behind her.

The class laughed again. Marta swivelled round on
her chair and banged her fist on the desk.

'Just because I can kick harder and faster than you!'

'Shut up, shorty!'

'Now, now!' said the teacher.

Marta hated being called 'shorty'. She hated it almost more than the football taunts. It was yet another difference to pick up on. She was the smallest in her class and slim-boned with it. If it wasn't her height they mentioned, they'd pick on her for being 'skinny' too.

Still, at least it was nearly time to go home. It had been a scorching hot day at school and Marta was wilting in the heat but she was staying at her grandmother's – who she called '*Avó*' – later. Afterwards, in the evening, as some of her family would arrive, her grandmother would serve up her delicious signature feijao dish: black beans soaked in onions, coriander and garlic, with meat picked up from the market. There wasn't a lot of it to share, but there was always just enough to go round. Her cousin José Roberto de Souza and his friends Valdemir Delfino da Silva and Luiz would arrive, and they normally let her sneak out with them for a game of football underneath the bridges.

That's where it had all started. She'd tagged along with them and watched and learnt from them. But it was when she got control of the ball that she'd discovered the power in her left foot. She felt free, racing at speed towards the goal, down whatever bit of pitch they'd created in the dust or dirt. They were baffled she enjoyed it so much but let her play. 'Just don't let your brothers find out!' they warned. Nobody in her family approved, least of all her elder brother, José.

The thought of her *Avó*'s feijao and the ball at her feet revived her. Sitting still in class felt torturous; her legs twitched as she did keepie-uppies in her head and she was told off by the teacher for constantly fidgeting. After school a group of girls trotted off to take dance classes. For a moment she wanted to be like them as they looked back at her and smirked, bursting into giggles down the corridor.

Maybe, Marta thought, life would be easier in the dance classes. She loved music and dancing. During the Carnival of Brazil festival before Easter, she and her family would all go down to the town square to hear the local samba band play, where they'd accompany them on *chocalho* (shakers) and *agogo* (bells). Her cousin had also taught her how to play a few bossa nova standards on guitar – 'Mas que nada' was her favourite. But she couldn't bear the sparkly outfits the girls wore for their dancing classes and the big shiny smiles they painted on for performances. She didn't really want to be looked at, or at least not while prancing about on a stage.

In any case, Marta felt as though she was dancing whenever her feet made contact with the ball. They came alive and did unexpected things – almost magical things she wasn't in control of, that always surprised her. But she knew it made her stand out in this town. And not in a good way.

CHAPTER 4

THE RIVERBED

'Marta?!' called her grandmother. 'Have you been in my sewing box again?'

'Er... what sewing box, *Avó*?' She quickly hid the handful of twisted old socks she'd been working into a ball to one side.

Her grandmother appeared, with a paper lunch bag in her hand.

'I think you know the one, Marta,' she replied with a disapproving look.

'Ah, thank you, *Avó*!' Marta reached out to take the leftover *fejaio*.

'Do not change the subject, Marta.' She wagged her finger at her. 'My supply of plastic bags appears to be going down rapidly too...'

'Hmm, that's strange, *Avó*...'

'Yes.'

Marta had begun to rely on a number of innovative methods for creating footballs. Cloth and paper were a poor substitute for the buoyancy of a real plastic football, but as a family they were used to making do. As long as she had a ball, that was the main thing.

Angela was standing by the door waiting for Marta. 'Come on, we need to go.' She tutted as she looked Marta up and down: 'Why do you not wear that dress that momma made? You're always in a T-shirt.'

'I can't play football in a dress!' Marta grumbled back at her. Although it wasn't easy playing in what she was wearing either. She relied on hand-me-downs from her older brothers, which meant T-shirts were often down to her knees and flying about. Still, it was always better than wearing a dress.

'But you can't play football now. We're going to school!' Angela protested.

A look of guilt flashed across Marta's face. 'Yeah, you go on ahead. I'll follow you.'

'Marta!'

'I will, I will.'

'Mum will go mad if she finds out.'

She would, too. But Marta had other ideas. She'd
heard her cousins whispering earlier about a dried-
up riverbed, just outside the main town centre.
Although the town prayed for rain and for water,
Marta found the dry riverbed perfect to run on. It
was also far from school – so there was no chance of
being spotted.

'Marta,' said her grandmother, 'you will be a good
girl won't you... you're heading straight to school
with your sister now.'

'Yes, *Avó*!' Marta replied. As soon as she'd turned
the corner of the street with Angela, she scrubbed
back her long black hair into a ponytail and sped off,
letting the ponytail swing wildly from side to side.

When she arrived her cousin José Roberto, and
Valdemir were lifting up heavy stones to form an
improvised goal.

Marta ran over to help.

'No, we can do it!'

26

'What's she doing here?' one of the boys asked. She recognised him as Davi, one of the lads who never passed the ball to her.

José Roberto and Valdemir looked uncomfortable as Marta strode over to Davi, folded her arms and looked up at his glaring eyes and furrowed expression. She was not fazed by his stare, even though he towered over her, and said, simply, 'I'm here to play.'

'Have you not found a dolly to play with yet?'

She looked up at him, shrugged and replied: 'No Davi, I got bored of playing with yours.'

He smirked.

At eight years old, Marta was one of the smallest girls in her year and had grown used to people towering over her, especially if they were a few years older than her, like Davi. But the comments still hurt, as much as she tried to make a joke out of them. She just wanted to play football – why was it such a big deal?

'Why are you always following us? Don't you know any girls to play with?' Davi said.

'They all think she's too macho for them!' another boy laughed.

'Yeah, you know what?' said a third. 'We don't want you playing with us today – run along now and play house.'

Marta felt her cheeks go red. But she was not going back. She'd run all this way to play. Despite her size, she was fast. But she always felt she had to run faster, just as she always knew she had to play better. She looked to Valdemir for support, and then to José Roberto. They both looked embarrassed. She knew if she lost her temper they'd jump on it immediately and call her a crybaby, but on this occasion she'd had enough.

'But I helped make the ball – this is so unfair!' She stamped her feet on the ground and felt hot tears spring to her eyes and her ponytail start to loosen.

'You see, this is why girls can't play, they just cry!' Davi mocked.

She felt her fists lash out and punch his stomach in frustration, and then felt José Roberto and Valdemir pulling her off him.

'Marta! Marta! Stop it!'

She looked at Davi with fury. He was laughing.

'You've got some fight in you, for a tiny one.'

'Oh come on then, let's just play,' said one other boy.

'Yeah come on, before the others turn up!' said José Roberto.

'I'll tell you what, she can play,' said Davi, 'but only if she scores in the first minute. If not, she has to go home.'

'Fine!' Marta shot back, not thinking for a second.

Valdemir looked at her.

'What? Easy!'

'Okay, go – prove it's easy!' shouted Davi.

CHAPTER 5

JUST ONE MINUTE

As they always did, they split the teams into a loose formation that was a world away from the strict, strategic style of play they watched on TV. Everyone's main aim was to get control of that ball and score, by any means possible. Whoever had possession of the ball could be marked by one or four opponents. And no-one wanted to be stuck in goal – whoever was nearest leapt in at the crucial point.

They all had a hunger for the ball when they played. But at this moment, Marta knew she'd have to demonstrate the biggest appetite.

Marta was tired of having to justify her love for football, but she wasn't about to give up now.

'Freak', 'Squirt', 'Unnatural' – she'd heard all the insults. And they did hurt. But right now, Marta knew the time for slinging mud back and forth had passed. Her words couldn't show them. But her feet could. Let them do the talking, she said to herself. Yes, I am a girl. Yes, I *can* play football. But I only have a minute to prove it.

In that single minute, Marta's bare feet barely touched the ground as they flew after the ball with speed, tenacity and ferocity. She was small but sturdy and was discovering that her size gave her an excellent sense of composure and balance. She outran each and every boy that challenged her, their feet desperately drumming against the cracked earth to keep up with her. She could hear their effort, their exhaustion, as she nimbly reached the ball and took control on one touch lifting it, spinning it, having fun with it as she took on each opponent desperate to get the ball off her. The boys never ever treated her like a girl when they played. And for that she was grateful.

One after another, they came at her, merciless

with their heel kicks, their shoves and their tugs. And it only made her faster, stronger, tougher. Her feet had to come up with new dribbles, new feints, new sleights to outfox and trick them, while she adjusted her pace to shock or surprise. Up ahead near goal she caught a glimpse of Davi's face sneering at her. Marta – focus, she told herself. Keep going. Don't stop now.

She accelerated at speed while keeping perfect control of the ball. There were two, maybe three, defenders hot on her heels. How much longer did she have left to prove it? She had no idea. She could see the two large stones marking the goal up ahead. First she had to deal with the opponent coming up on her right. The cries of her cousins were ringing in her ears as she toe-kicked the ball with her strongest left foot up over his head, before fetching it on the other side. She then smashed the ball well within the two stones with her left foot, but not before catching a glimpse of Davi's bewildered expression as he lurched to the right of the goal and flailed to the floor.

GOAL!!! Oh – the joy she felt as Valdemir and José Roberto lifted her tiny frame onto their shoulders and the rest of the team jumped around her.

'Did I do it? Did I do it in time??' She wanted to know.

Davi, bright red and fuming was staring at her, just shaking his head. There was her answer. He mouthed 'freak' at her, but she didn't care. At this moment, it felt pretty good to be a freak.

Her joy was short-lived, though. As she walked back in the afternoon sun, and was nearly home, she caught sight of her mother talking to a group of women – one of whom she recognised as Davi's mother, talking in excited tones. Her heart sank as familiar words and phrases jumped out at her.

'...not normal...'

'It's odd for a girl to be playing...'

'Too macho...'

'Why do you let her do that?'

And then she heard her mum say what she always said in response: 'Leave her alone, just let her be... let her be...'

'Oh not again...'

Marta walked past with her head down trying not to be noticed, but not before catching sight of her mother's disappointed and hurt face. Her mum always stuck up for her but Marta felt guilty and frustrated that her love of football caused her

mum this grief. She wished she lived in a town where other girls played, so there wasn't this constant fight and fuss to do what she loved. She knew her mother had enough on her plate to deal with. But there was also a part of her that wished her mum could spend more time with her or watch her play. Then maybe she could share in the joy she felt.

Finally, Marta was home. She rushed through the front door and avoided saying hello to Angela. If she could whizz out again in time and head to her *Avó*'s, maybe she could catch her cousins for another quick game on the scrubland.

But before she could go anywhere, her mum cornered her.

'Young lady, were you at school today?'

'Umm... I need to go Mum, *Avó* wants me to help her with the chickens tonight...'

'Marta! Look me in the eye and answer the question.'

'Mãe... I'm sorry...'

Tereza looked at her wearily. 'This has got to stop. I don't want you to do this anymore. It upsets me.'

'But Mãe... why?'

'It upsets all of us. None of us understand why you want to do this.'

'Because I love football, Mãe, I love playing...'

'But everyone is *so* mean to you when you play...'

Marta looked at her mum. She understood – Tereza just wanted to protect her, her baby. And her brothers felt the same towards their little baby sister.

'I know, Mãe...' And she felt the tears spring up in her eyes.

'Can't you find something you'd enjoy? You could take dance lessons with Angela in the church... or hula hooping... or hairdressing! You have such beautiful hair – it would look so lovely in a plait!'

'But Mãe, football is my dancing! And you know what – I'm good at it! If you saw me play... you'd see!'

'I see you play with the boys. I don't like it, look at the bruises you get!' She grabbed her arm.

'I don't care! I'm good enough to do the Peladão tournament one day!' As she said it, Marta's eyes lit up at the thought. She'd heard stories from older players in the neighbourhood who'd played at the annual amateur competition.

Her mother scoffed. 'How? In the beauty pageant?! You'll need to start behaving very differently if you want to do that!'

Marta thought of the girls who just stood around in bikinis at the Peladão tournament, looking pretty. She couldn't even begin to imagine doing that.

Her mother continued. 'They'd never let you take part! Because you are not a boy, Marta!'

'No! But I wish I was! Then maybe everyone would just leave me alone!'

Marta ran out through the door with her mother calling after her.

The sun was dipping in the sky, setting off beautiful colours all across the scrubland. Marta thought of her family and imagined what it would be like to stop playing. Yes, it would make life a lot easier. But it would also be a lot more joyless. There was nothing else she really wanted to do, nothing else she could imagine herself doing. Maybe there was another way out of this town other than football.

What could she do? She saw girls not that much older than Angela settling down, getting married and having children. A life of that stretched ahead her, living hand to mouth in this town, struggling to feed her children. And there were certainly no boys she wanted to marry in this town – ugh!

Suddenly, she remembered something her teacher at Sunday School had said: 'God gives everyone a special talent. *Everyone.*' Marta knew that her mum would love it more if that special talent was needlework or embroidery. But it wasn't. Anyway, would God give her this talent if she wasn't meant to use it? It was ridiculous. Why waste it on her? Why not just give it to another boy?

Marta said aloud to herself: 'I want to do this. I'm going to do this.' She started laughing at how strong her conviction was. But deep down she knew it was true. She had no idea how she was going to do it, or where it would take her. But she had to keep going. 'Just keep showing up, just keep playing.'

CHAPTER 6

BETTER THAN THE BOYS

There was a festival feeling in the air. It was a baking hot late afternoon, and Marta and her friends had gathered to cheer on the local Dois Riachos football team, who were playing against the neighbouring town of Santana do Ipanema. In the crowd, people were banging out samba beats on drums, upturned bins and boxes, or anything else they could get their hands on.

How Marta longed to play in a local team or an actual league, and have the chance to represent her own town doing what she loved. She didn't dare share these thoughts – she kept them to herself because she knew her cousins and friends would laugh at her. But she was always dreaming.

She dreamed of flying down a pitch with the ball at her feet, cutting past defenders while her hometown cheered her on, of feeling euphoria as the goal opened up before her, with the ball still tightly controlled at her feet – then boom! She dreamed of everyone cheering and hugging her. No-one pulled faces or made comments. And she dreamed of knowing that when she looked into the crowd her mother, grandmother, sister and brothers would all be there smiling and laughing.

Suddenly, her daydreams were interrupted. She realised one of the players had lost control of the ball and it was soaring off the pitch. Her face lit up. She and the other kids loved it when this happened, because they had a chance to get control of the ball and kick it back on to the pitch for play.

Marta didn't even look to see who she was up against, as she sped towards the ball. She had only one mission in mind – to reach it before the others. She felt her bare feet thud and pound against the earth. She heard José shouting, 'Get it, get it,

Valdemir!' None of this distracted her – it only made her more determined. Nor was she deterred by the boy who was constantly trying to push her out of the way. She stuck her right foot forward, kicked the ball up into the air on first touch, caught it with her knees, and keepie-uppied with it for a second or two. Finally she slammed it back onto the pitch at the player, who was hollering at her to pass. She beamed at him as he shouted: 'Thanks, little lady!'

It wasn't long before she was encircled by a chorus of groans and insults:

'You let a girl get it??'

'What?? Who let her that close to the pitch?'

'Oh it's her again – macho girl!'

Marta struggled to get her breath back again. José was at her side.

'Marta, couldn't you have let me get it?'

'Oh, whatever!' Marta groaned, as she turned away from a sea of angry stares. In the distance, however, she spotted a man watching her with bemused interest. He wore a blue tracksuit and football cap with the local team colours on it and his eyes were kind and twinkling. He smiled and waved: 'Great kick, kid!'

Marta was so shocked to hear these positive words she wondered if they were even meant for her. She barely knew where to look and even pulled a slight grimace as she realised the man was talking to her.

At half-time the boys ran off to set up a team. Marta followed them.

They turned around. 'Marta...'

'Oh, come on...'

One of them pointed to a group of local boys on the sidelines. 'Why don't you play with them?'

Marta looked over. She'd played with them before and knew they weren't particularly good.

As ever, she shrugged. She never wanted to show them they'd got to her. 'Fine, I'll play whoever.'

She ran over to them.

'Julio! Saville! Who wants to play?'

'Come on, you – we need another five for a proper game! Who wants to defend?' 'Why don't you get in goal?'

It was hard for them to ignore Marta, even if she

was a girl. She spoke with such excitement and authority. One by one she rallied the boys together into a team, but not before ordering them to find a couple of upturned drums to sketch out a penalty area.

'Let's do this properly!'

'But that's not a proper ball!' they all pointed out, staring at her latest paper-bag-and-cloth construction.

'So what?! Quit your whining!'

As usual, it didn't take long for Marta to be in possession of the ball. Her balance, coupled with her speed and agility, allowed her to retain control even when some of the larger players put pressure on her. She felt their surprise, sense of awe and even a little fear as she dropped her shoulders, swivelled her hips and dragged the ball around opponents without it ever leaving her foot. She forgot all the catty comments of the afternoon, as she scored goal after goal, unable to contain her delight at the fact the boys were marvelling at her quick pace and equally quick-thinking brain.

CHAPTER 7

OPPORTUNITY KNOCKS

But her mood would change when she arrived home that evening. She opened the door to the disappointed faces of her mother and José.

'Sit down Marta,' said José.

Marta didn't like the serious tone in her elder brother's voice.

'What is it? Mãe?'

He continued. 'You're almost eleven now. A young lady. Your mother and I have decided it's time you helped out more. Like your sister does.'

'I need you to start bringing in some income, Marta. I'd like you to help your sister on the market at the weekends,' her mother said.

'Both days?'

'Yes.'

Marta knew what this meant: no time at the weekends to watch matches with her cousins or play football.

'But Mãe! Is this because I went to the match today?'

'No whining, Marta!' said José. 'It is time you took some responsibility. We can't have you running about like you're a boy. It's embarrassing for us! People talk!'

'Mãe!' pleaded Marta. 'I want to help you more, of course I do! I'm happy to work in the market but please, please let me have some time to play football!'

'Oh Marta, I don't know,' replied Tereza.

'Don't be soft on her, Mother.'

Marta felt tears well up in her yet again, tears of frustration, at this continuous battle.

Suddenly there was a light knock at the door and a friendly sounding 'Hello!' They were used to neighbours and cousins traipsing in and out so it was rare for anyone to shout out a greeting.

Tereza frowned as she saw a man standing at the door. Marta recognised him straight away as the man from the local match who'd admired her footwork.

'I hope I'm not intruding – is this a bad time?' He was still in his tracksuit and was mopping his brow.

Tereza was worried. 'It's not Valdir, is it?'

'Oh no...'

'He's not skipping school as well, is he?' asked José.

'No, I... I came to see this young lady, actually.'

Marta looked down. Oh no, what was he going to say? She braced herself for another mean or sly comment – was he going to have a go at her mum and ask her why she allowed her to embarrass the family at local games? It was the last thing she needed.

'My name is Tota, I work at the local municipal and manage the under-14s local junior team in Dois Riachos.'

Tereza sighed. 'Have you spotted her playing

football when she should be at school? I know, I know... I'm sorry, I just don't have the time to watch her all the time. She tells me she's going to school but what can I do? I have to go out and work. If I didn't, maybe then I could stop her from playing football.'

'But why would you want to do that?' said Tota.

Marta looked up in surprise while her mother looked confused.

'She's so good at it!' he went on.

Marta felt herself go bright red.

'She's got a lot of spirit – for one so tiny! Something of a Baixinho!'

Marta felt herself go redder. It meant 'shorty' but was widely known as star Brazilian player Romario's nickname.

Tota addressed both Tereza and José. 'I hope you don't mind me coming to see you but I saw her playing at the local match today. I think she's got a lot of potential.'

He laughed, and continued: 'And a lot of determination. Does she get that from you?'

They both looked flummoxed.

José spoke first. 'We do not want to encourage her. She should not be playing football.'

'Why?'

'It's not right,' said Tereza.

'Says who?'

They were both suddenly stumped for an answer.

Tota turned back to an astonished Marta. 'You like setting up games don't you?'

'Everywhere I go!' she said.

'How would you like to try out for the local Dois Riachos team?'

'What??' Marta's mouth fell open.

'I'd like to see a bit more of what that left foot can do. With even more training and discipline.'

'Me? You want me?' She laughed for a second. 'You don't mind I'm a girl?'

'I want good footballers – that's what I want.'

Marta couldn't believe her ears. Someone had noticed her talent positively and wasn't making her feel weird or different for it. Sure, she knew her cousin José Roberto recognised her talent, but she was so used to hearing 'macho girl' ringing in her ears. To meet someone who saw her as a footballer, not just a girl playing football, was a revelation.

But as she turned and looked at her mother's alarmed face, she knew she had a long way to go in making her happy about it.

Tereza and José started to ask questions: 'What does this mean for her?'; 'How often would she play?'; 'Can she still work on the market?'

'If she makes it onto the team she'll play weekends, some evenings.'

'Oh please Mãe, please!' said Marta. 'Let me try out! I'll still work on the market – I promise!'

Tereza shook her head. 'I don't know, I don't know.'

'Have you seen your daughter play?' Tota asked her.

'No, not really... well, I... I know she can do it...'

'She has something that all the great Brazilian players have – that love for the game, that hunger, Dona... er...'

'Vieira da Silva.'

'Have you seen how happy she is when she plays? Does it really matter what other people say?'

'Okay... okay!' Tereza relented. 'I don't think I could stop her anyway.'

'Thank you, Mãe!' Marta jumped up and kissed her.

CHAPTER 8

"BUT SHE'S A GIRL!"

While the rest of the local boys' junior team got ready for the game in the sports ground's locker room, Marta was changing into her football gear in the small toilet area next door.

The other boys in the team had objected strongly to her sharing a locker room with them. 'No! She's a girl!' They'd looked her up and down as if she was a completely foreign animal.

She'd laughed in response – 'Believe me, I don't want to share one with you either!' – and waved her hand in front of her nose in an exaggerated way, pretending to cough and gag. As she always did, whenever faced with a put-down for being a girl, she made a joke and shrugged it off.

'Now, now,' said Tota, 'she's one of you when you're out there playing – leave her alone. We're here to win, right? And beat the other team – yes?'

'Yes, Tota...' they all groaned in unison.

Marta smiled at him gratefully. He always had her back in these situations.

She was playing in a five-a-side indoor team and they were about to face their rivals Santana do Ipanema. Although they hailed from only 20 km west of Dois Riachos, they could have come from another planet.

The pitch in the hall was a completely different environment to the scrublands she was used to playing on. Although she was very excited to have passed the tryouts and been accepted onto the team, it felt strange not to feel the earth beneath her feet. And she did feel lonely, tucked away in a toilet, away from the camaraderie of the rest of the team.

She looked down at her oversized football shirt with its yellow and purple colours. It was at least two sizes too big, reaching down well past her knees, almost like a dress. They couldn't afford to get a new one in her size, not that Marta would ask her mum – it was quite miraculous she was being allowed to play and she'd been used to bigger-sized clothes all her life anyway.

Although she always felt a little ridiculous as she tucked her jersey into boys' shorts, which she also had to tighten with a piece of string, she still felt proud wearing a kit. She wasn't wearing some torn or ragged overgrown T-shirt handed down from Angela or Valdir – so surely this meant she had to be taken a bit more seriously, right? Her skills had got her here – meaning a cramped toilet, she chuckled to herself – and she was closer than ever to finding acceptance as a football player.

Tota knocked on the door.

'Are you ready, Marta?'

'You bet!'

She opened the door and sprang out, giving Tota a huge smile. Her dark eyes flashed with steely determination. Tota almost pitied any defender who had the misfortune to lock eyes with Marta. They might tower over her but she was like a wall that they couldn't get past, round or over. It was a joy to see her develop into an extremely creative centre-forward and she always had the mentality of a winner.

Santana do Ipanema wouldn't know what had hit them when she was out there.

As Marta jogged into the hall she saw the same looks and stares that she always got. She'd been playing in the team for a while, but there were the usual sniggers and gasps from the opposing team, and she saw a sea of confused and puzzled expressions from parents in the stands.

Just do what you always do, she said to herself, don't try and justify, don't try and please. Pretend this is like any other game you played on the scrublands – and you can feel the hot earth beneath your bare feet. Just show them on the pitch.

Marta sized up the opposition straight away and started plotting her moves three plays down, already assessing which defenders she could take on. The whistle blew for kick-off and she sped off down the pitch into spaces she could get ready to attack from and receive passes.

She picked up a ball at first touch, outrunning an opponent on the way. The ball felt as light as a feather as she dribbled at speed towards one defender, turning this way and that to confuse him on her direction. The cries, whoops and gasps of delight from the auditorium morphed into the background as she took on another defender, dancing with the ball for a few seconds before nudging it through his legs and picking it up again.

In the penalty area, another defender attempted to dismantle her, but she was too fast with her twists and turns around him. The goal opened up for her and she saw the keeper make a desperate attempt to decipher what her feet were up to. She slowed for a split second before deciding where to slam the ball with her left foot – into the top right of the net.

GOAL!!! Her teammates whooped and danced around her. She'd scored within the first five minutes.

'Go Marta – go!' She saw Tota at the sidelines with his fists in the air.

Marta went on to shoot one more goal and set up two assists – every time she played she felt her feet and her confidence soaring. But when they beat Santana 3–1 she could hear boos rising up around the hall, among the cheers of jubilation. She knew they were aimed at her and felt her head fall.

She saw Tota turn to them.

'Shame on you! What bad losers!' he cried. 'You are adults – not children!'

Marta often saw Tota react this way after they'd won a match. Although she appreciated him sticking up for her, she felt embarrassed by the negative attention, as though she was responsible for spoiling the atmosphere.

She headed back to the toilet to change, feeling defeated, even though they'd won. Would this ever change?

CHAPTER 9

NEW BOOTS AND HOME BATTLES

'Marta!' She heard Tota call. She stopped and turned around.

'Come on, don't be discouraged,' he said. 'You played so well today.'

'I know.' She said it simply, her eyes staring at him with their usual defiance. Even so, she cursed herself as she felt the same familiar tears come to the surface.

He took her by the shoulders and looked her in the eyes.

'Come on, Baixinho, you gave it your all out there.'

'I have to. I always have to. I can never slack off. I

always have to prove I play as well as the boys. And even then – they hate me!'

She felt the tears pouring down her cheeks.

'Marta, you play better than the boys. Better. I shouldn't say this, but you're better than a lot of them – your technical ability for one so young is incredible. You could be another Romario, Ronaldinho, even your favourite – Rivaldo.'

'Do you think I could have the chance to be a professional footballer?'

She saw the doubt cross his face.

'I hope so, Marta. You certainly deserve to. But whatever happens, don't ever lose your joy for playing.'

Marta smiled, her spirits lifting.

'Now look,' he said. 'I got you something... they're not perfect... but, I knew you'd play well today...'

He pulled out a pair of football boots from his bag. Marta gasped in amazement. They were unbranded, worn down a little at the backs and clearly too big, by at least three sizes. But they were an actual pair of football boots, complete with studs at the bottom.

'My first pair of cleats!' she shouted excitedly.

'Try them on!'

Marta pulled off her plimsolls and put her feet into the boots. It was obvious her feet were swimming about in them. She saw Tota's face fall.

'Ah... oh they're a little on the big side... I can return them?'

'No, they're perfect,' she shot back straight away.

'Really?'

'Thank you Tota – thank you!'

When she arrived home she found some paper, rolled it up and stuffed some into the end of each shoe. She then slipped her feet back into them and ran over to her grandmother's, kicking up dust as she sprinted over wasteland, feeling as though everything was just right with the world.

'Look, look!' she sambaed around the kitchen, swaying her hips. 'Look at my cleats!' I love them!'

'They are a gift from God,' said her grandmother, smiling widely.

Later, when he saw the boots, Valdemir said to Marta, 'Wow! You're even happier about them than you are about winning the game today!'

Yes, she was. Because she knew she would go on to win many more games wearing them. And with these on her feet, she began to believe that her dream of becoming a professional player could come true.

'Mãe!!!' Marta came flying through the door, nearly knocking the crucifix off the wall that hung above it.

'Marta! Careful!'

'I've been picked! They want me – they want me!!!'

'Calm down, Marta – who wants you?!'

'I cannot be calm, Mãe – I cannot be *calm!*' Marta ran out to the yard and started doing scissor kicks.

'CSA wants me! The youth system!'

'*The* Centro Sportivo Alagoano? In Maceió?'

'Yes! The biggest club in the whole state of Alagoas – with the most fans!'

'Oh Marta! That is amazing!'

'You know it's where Dida came from? Before he went to Flamengo? He was a forward too! And their second highest scorer! One day I'm gonna run rings around Clube de Regatas, too!'

Tereza looked at her, a little forlornly.

'You really want to do this, don't you?'

'Well, of course, Mãe.'

'I know you love it Marta, I know, I see that – although I find it hard to understand at times. For some reason God has given you this gift... but... I fear you can only go so far with it.'

'Far? Far? I'm going all the way... first Maceió, then Rio!'

'Oh Marta! Please – stop dreaming!'

Marta stared at her defiantly.

'I'll do it, Mãe, I will, you'll see.'

'This is a hobby, Marta, you can't do this forever. You'll have to settle down one day and find a normal job...'

'A normal job? What? Here? What is there for me to do here? It's happening, Mum, I just know it. And just think – when I'm making money from football I can help you. Much more than I do just working on the market...'

'Oh Marta, that's sweet, but it's not going to happen, they won't let you...'

'Who's "they"?'

'I don't want you to get your hopes up, my dear, and have them shattered. You must remember who you are. You are a girl. They are not going to forget that.'

'Yes, Mama. I am a girl. A girl called Marta. Who will be a famous footballer one day! And that is what *they* will remember me for!'

'*Minha nossa!*' Tereza sighed. She looked up to the sky and made the '*sinal da cruz*' – the sign of the cross – and rolled her eyes.

CHAPTER 10

UNION AND STRENGTH

Marta was up early, to train with Tota, ahead of CSA's game on Saturday in the regional cup – the first game to kick off the tournament. Although he didn't coach her directly anymore, he continued to support her.

'It's important you don't get complacent, Marta,' he said, 'just because you're playing for CSA now.'

'Hey! You know how seriously I have to take this, Tota. I can't afford to put a foot wrong.'

She knew she always had to play her absolute best – she knew she played better than most of the lads on the team and she'd been singled out as one of their top players. But still the fear remained at the back of her mind that she could be accused of not being good enough.

'Okay Marta, let's warm up and stretch.'

'Tota, I've already done that. I was here twenty minutes before you. I want to practise the Elastico.'

She'd seen Ronaldinho employ the Elastico on the field and it had become one of her favourite dribbling moves to outwit players – using her quick feet to move deftly in and around the ball to fool defenders on the direction she was taking. Ronaldinho, the young Number 10, was fast becoming one of her favourites and she worked hard to emulate him.

Her technical skills, control of the ball and ability to strike on target were sharpening all the time, along with her quick-thinking mind. She felt less resentful about always playing with boys because they helped her to run and dribble even faster.

At CSA she wore the Number 7 shirt, which gave her opportunities to dominate the midfield and strike on the right wing with her powerful left boot. She knew, as Tota had always also predicted, that she could disrupt the opposition in almost any position. But she really longed to play in the coveted striker position – she knew she could be at her most creative on the attack.

'It's always about the goals, isn't it Tota? There's no point otherwise.'

He laughed. 'Absolutely, Marta. You play to win.'

Marta could see her cousin José Roberto, Valdemir Delfino and Tota in the crowd as she ran out onto the pitch for CSA's home game against Fluminense Football Club from Rio. She wore her blue-and-white kit with the team's logo '*União e força*' (Union and Strength) written across it. Yes, the shirt was still flapping around her knees and she could feel her feet rubbing against the paper wedged in her cleats, but her heart was beating with pride as she heard Delfino shout out 'Come on, Marta!'

She saw the other parents cheering on their kids – some of whom she recognised from her church in Dois Riachos. Her heart sank for a minute. It was at times like these she wished her dad or mum could be there. But hey, her cousins were there, the people she'd played with and learnt from, and that's all that mattered. They still teased her a little and called her 'macho girl', but she felt deep down they were finally accepting her talent and were proud of her.

She still felt some animosity from her team players, though, and she knew their coach Alberto had picked up on it. Before the game he gathered them together in the locker room.

'Okay, we've made it halfway through the tournament – let's keep up the good work, guys! But we need to remember that we're a team, right? Remember our logo – strength is important but we need unity too! We can be even stronger then!'

'Martim,' Alberto went on, 'when you see Marta running up on that right side – you *must* pass to her, okay? You know she can pick it up.'

'Uh huh.'

Marta sighed. She knew Martim always wanted to take the strikes for himself but often missed.

'Mattias – pass to Marta if she's near the penalty box, she can create chances once she's in there.'

It was deflating to Marta that they always had to

have these conversations before a match, but she'd seen the envy in her teammates' eyes when she grasped the chance to plough down defenders. Once the huddle was over she looked at Alberto and said: 'If they pass to me, we'll win.'

'Don't worry about winning for now... just get out there and play.' He paused for a second before saying, 'Marta, you know... it's because...'

'I'm a girl?'

'A girl, who is exceptionally good.'

Yes, which meant that every goal she scored or set up was a little bit tainted – not as special as when one of the other players scored. The pitch was still a lonely place. Which is why she reminded herself, every time she ran out onto the pitch: Why would God give me this talent if he didn't want me to use it? With that thought to guide her, she felt calmer, more at peace, and not so alone anymore.

Fluminense Football Club was known for its tough players and, as usual, they were older and taller than she was. They had a couple of strong strikers too and one scored within the first twenty minutes. Marta knew that she could get through them, though, if more passes came her way.

Just before half-time she had a chance. One of the opposing midfielders lost control of the ball. She picked it up and saw some space open down the pitch. She nudged it to José Roberto who was on the wing, then ran forward into the penalty area, outrunning a defender who was hot on her heels.

'Pass! Pass!'

Her angle was deep but she knew she could go for a shot on either foot. She picked up the ball on first touch from Martim, just before another defender reached her. In his effort to block, he fell to the floor. She barely looked for the goalkeeper as she slammed it hard with her right foot. She looked back, almost in disbelief as she saw it smash into the top left of the goal.

They had equalised. Waves of euphoria and relief washed over her as the whistle blew for half-time. She felt the arms of her teammates around her shoulders and heard the cheers of her family in the crowd.

'Great play, Marta – great play!' Alberto congratulated her at half-time. Marta could not stop beaming. She felt the rising irritation of her teammates as the coach praised her, but was amazed when Martim said: 'You know what, Marta – that was one of the best goals we've scored this season.'

Marta was tempted to shoot back that '*I've* scored' but she didn't. She was more amazed that this was one of the first times he'd addressed her as Marta, not 'macho-girl'. It was almost strange to hear her name spoken aloud by one of her teammates. 'Yes. "Marta",' she thought, 'my name.'

That first goal had raised their spirits. Marta felt the team relax in the second half and there was a better flow of communication. The opposition's striker scored a second goal but Marta set up an assist for José Roberto, then shot the winning goal ten minutes from the end. They were through to the next round of the regional cup to play Esporte Clube Barroso, one of the best teams in Alagoas.

After the match Marta was presented with a medal for 'Player of the Match'. It was a gold-plated football with a striker in the middle. The strap was decorated with the colours of the team. Marta gasped with delight as she rushed off to show Valdemir and José Roberto, trying to hold back the tears. Not even the sulky looks of her teammates, or the fact the player in the medal was clearly a boy, could spoil her enjoyment of this prize.

'Marta, you're just getting better and better!' Valdemir said.

'Our little shorty!' cried José.

They'd made it halfway through the tournament and Marta knew it wouldn't be long until she was lifting the regional cup for Dois Riachos. Nothing else mattered to her.

CHAPTER 11

BACK ON THE MARKET

Marta knew that something was up the second she opened the door. It was Alberto. He looked crestfallen and couldn't look her in the eye.

Marta gulped.

'What is it?'

He started to garble. 'I'm so sorry Marta... You see, I have no real choice really... the coach from Esporte Clube Barroso says he won't play... there's nothing I can do.'

He couldn't look her in the eye.

'We're going to have to pull you from the tournament, Marta.'

Marta felt her stomach lurch and panic set in.

'Why?' she asked.

'The other team's coach has threatened to pull out if you play. Because of this the championship organiser has decided it would be better if you... stepped out... We're so far in now, you see, we can't really drop out... It's for the good of the team. You do understand, don't you Marta?'

'No, no, I really don't! This is so unfair!' Marta felt her fists clenching. 'What did he say? This coach? What was his reason?'

'This isn't a place for girls.'

'But... I've done so well... I got a medal... I'm the top player, you said that, right??'

'I know, I know... but this coach... I'm afraid, he has a lot of clout... if he pulls out we could lose further sponsorship. I do have to think of the team's future...'

Yes of course, thought Marta. No-one would think of her future, no-one would fight for her, even though she was good enough. 'It's because the boys feel inferior, isn't it? Because I'm better than them. You need me on that team! You won't win without me!'

'It's out of my hands... I'm sorry... but hey, look, I have some good news. There might be a local girls' team starting up... how about you join them?'

Marta slammed the door in his face. She didn't want him to see her cry.

*

On the day of the match, Marta stood selling fruit at the market. She was grumpy and couldn't hide it as she thrust bananas and grapefruits into paper bags.

'You're scaring the customers,' said Angela. 'Try and smile.'

Marta glared back at her furiously. The words 'this isn't a place for girls' were still ringing in her head.

Well, *this* wasn't a place for her either. And the thought of being stuck here trying to smile, while her former teammates got to play football, left her feeling miserable. Her mum was right though. They had stopped her. They had only let her go so far. They were winning.

'Marta?' She heard a voice she didn't recognise. It was a softer dialect than the local accent – the speaker wasn't from nearby.

Marta looked up from the till, into the face of a smiling woman. 'Yes?'

How did this woman know her name? She didn't look like one of her mum's friends. She was a bit too well-dressed and was wearing make-up. Marta caught a whiff of perfume.

The woman held out her hand. Marta pulled a face. This was strange.

'My name is Helena. I'm from Vasco da Gama.'

Marta stared blankly.

'You've heard of it?'

'Yes, of course,' said Marta. Everyone had heard of it. It was one of the biggest clubs in Rio de Janeiro.

'One of my scouts saw you play in the match against Esporte Clube Barroso. Could we talk?'

'Er...' Marta looked over at Angela, who was staring at her quizzically.

'How would you like to try out for them?' said Helena. 'I want to put together a women's team in Rio and we think you'd be ideal.'

Marta's mouth fell open and she dropped the pallet of grapefruits she'd had ready in her hands to re-stock. She scrabbled to pick them up as they rolled around all over the place. Helena bent down to help her.

'Thanks... thanks...' said Marta, still in complete disbelief.

'Oh, and please, could I have a bunch of your best local bananas?'

CHAPTER 12

HEADING FOR RIO

'But it's so far away!' Tereza sat on the porch of their house in the evening sun with José Roberto and Valdemir, her head in her hands.

'It's only a few days on a bus. She'll be fine,' Valdemir said.

'It's three days! My baby, alone on a bus for three days?' Tereza wailed.

'This could be an amazing chance for her.'

'She's still only a young girl.'

'She's fourteen, she won't be a girl for long. She'll have to think about her prospects soon. She's not getting a proper education here – we can't even afford to send her to school.'

'I've never even been to Rio!' said Tereza. 'What if something happens to her?'

'She'll be perfectly safe staying with my cousin Marcos and his family,' said José Roberto. 'They are good people – I promise they'll look after her and won't let her come to any harm.'

'It's Marcos who's helped set up the try-out,' said Valdemir. 'She could be back within a few weeks if she doesn't make it.'

'At least let her try, Aunt Tereza.'

'Are there actually other girls playing football then?' Tereza said. She was puzzled.

'Yes,' laughed Valdemir. 'Believe it or not, there are girls in Brazil – in fact, girls all over the world – who want to play. That's why they're trying to put women's teams together at Fluminense and Vasco. She'll have opportunities there she'd never have here.'

He added: 'We all think she could really make something of herself out there.'

'But what if they're mean to her?'

'People have been mean to her all her life.'

'But she won't have her family, we can't protect her here.'

Valdemir shrugged.

'She's tough, Tereza. God knows, she's had to be.'

Tereza shook her head. 'I don't know – how can we afford a trip like that anyway?'

'All taken care of. Marcos can lend us the money, we'll pay it back when we can.'

Tereza sighed. 'I've known for a long time I can't stop her.'

'What have you always said, Tereza? Leave it in God's hands. If she's meant to be there...'

*

Marta stood at the bus station in Dois Riachos, feeling sick with nerves. Her eyes looked up, bewildered by all the destinations flashing up on the screens. It was a small station but a gateway to many different cities – some she'd never ever heard of, such as Curitiba and Goiânia.

Valdemir, José Roberto and Luiz were with her at the bus station to see her off. She'd already said her goodbyes to Mãe and the rest of her family at home.

In her hands she clasped a necklace of St
Christopher, the patron saint of travellers, in her hand.

'But Mãe – I can't take this!' Marta had told
Tereza. It was her mother's favourite.

'Marta, he will help you get to Rio,' said Tereza.
'And wherever you go from there.'

Marta had faltered at that point. Did she really
have to go? Could she go?

As José Roberto scanned the boards to check
which gate her bus was boarding from, her stomach
started to churn. The reality of sitting on that bus
alone taking the long journey out of the only city
and home she'd ever known hit her. What was she
thinking? Who was she trying to kid? She'd been told
all her life she couldn't play, shouldn't play, was this
some sort of joke?

What if she got to Rio and her skills suddenly
vanished and she returned as a laughing stock? That
would show her, they'd all say. She'd awoken with
a start in the night from dreams where her body
suddenly froze on the pitch, opponents outrunning
her while she remained stuck, unable to get control

of the ball as it rolled further and further away from her.

She suddenly wished more than anything that the bus was cancelled or, better still, that a giant dust devil would arrive wreaking havoc on the bus station and she would have a wonderful excuse not to go through with any of this. So she could just stay 'macho girl' forever. She could always wait to find out who this other girl Marta was.

She lifted her satchel, full to the brim with her favourite snacks – pão de queijo (cheese bread) and cassava chips. She felt the weight of her new football boots, stuffed at the bottom of her bag, that José Roberto had bought for her – a reminder of where she was going and what she was about to do.

'So you look the part, Marta, like a professional,' said José Roberto. These were actually branded – Adidas – and fitted her properly. Still, she couldn't help feeling as though she was betraying the old pair Tota had given her.

'It's departing from gate number five,' said José Roberto. 'Are you ready?'

Marta shook her head.

He put his arm round her. 'Within a week you'll have forgotten all about this place, about us.'

'Rio de Janeiro!' The call came.

José Roberto and Valdemir hugged her goodbye.

'Please swim in the Rodrigo de Freitas lagoon for us, Marta!'

'Just think of all those beautiful things you're going to see!'

Marta's mouth felt dry and her palms started to sweat.

'Get on the bus, Marta.'

Marta's hand shook as she handed her ticket to the driver and climbed the steps up into the bus.

'Where do I sit?'

'Oh, anywhere you like,' said the driver.

As the engine started up Marta chose not to look back out of the window at José Roberto and Valdemir. She was scared she might suddenly jump up and demand the bus screech to a stop as it was pulling out of the station. It was a long way to Rio – 1,000 miles. But with each mile that passed she knew it would be much harder to turn back. Just take it, one mile at a time, one day at a time, she told herself.

As they travelled through her home state of Alagoas the flat, brown and barren roads slowly gave way to green countryside. On the second day of the journey they passed through the state of Bahia, where she caught glimpses of the tropical coast in the distance, before arriving in the city of Salvador with its stunning colonial architecture. She looked out in amazement as they approached the mountains of Belo Horizonte that curved around the city, before catching a glimpse of Mineirão Stadium and Lake Pampulha. She could see now why Belo Horizonte was named 'beautiful horizon'. The bulk of the main journey was over. Rio was only another six hours away.

Mãe had given her a pillow to sleep on but the seats were not the comfiest and Marta was too full of adrenaline to really switch off. She managed to doze off periodically and awoke bleary-eyed to see the outstretched arms of Cristo Redentor across the Corcovado mountain.

She sat up with a start. Wow! She had seen pictures of the statue, but to see it in the flesh was incredible, as the sunrise began to light up the entire city and set the waters shimmering across Guanabara Bay. Her heart skipped a beat as the driver gave the call for Rio and the bus swung into the station. It wasn't long before she spotted Marcos, looking out for her eagerly. She had arrived!

CHARLOTTE BROWNE

CHAPTER 13

THE BIG CITY

Marta lay awake that night, on a cot in the living room of Marcos's family home, her new base. Although she was exhausted from the bus journey she couldn't sleep. The sounds and smells of the city were all so new and strange to her and she realised with a pang she missed the familiar sounds of home – Angela singing, rubbish floating about in the backyard and the sound of cicadas.

Now she was several storeys up in a building, just one of many other hundreds of flats stacked high in a city of millions. Sirens blared and cars honked on the streets below her, and she heard a high-pitched scream from somewhere.

She knew that Marcos had let the coach know she'd arrived, but it felt strange to wait to play football. She looked at her new boots, as if they were waiting in the corner, and almost longed for her old pair back home. She thought of all the matches they'd seen her through. She knew she had to look the part with her new Adidas branded trainers but would she have the confidence to match?

In her first week, she went running in them every day along the beach, to prepare for her chance on the pitch, listening to bossa nova jazz guitarists jamming in the bars. But she was still itching to feel a football at her feet again.

Why had the club not called? Had they decided she wasn't worth their while? Just a girl from the backwaters they didn't want on the team? She missed her family but also wondered how she'd break it to them if she had to come home again.

'Be patient,' said Marcos's wife. 'They'll call for you. They probably have a lot of girls to see.'

Early one afternoon she came back from the beach and heard Marcos on the phone.

'Ah... I think she's just come in... Marta?'

Marta stared at him, almost too petrified to take the receiver.

'Hello?'

'Marta? This is Helena from Vasco da Gama. Can you come down to the stadium today?'

'Yes!' Marta heard her voice squeak, before she hung up and sprinted out the door.

When she got there, she was struck by a sight she'd never seen before: a field of women playing football. Not getting stared at, or whispered about. Just out there, playing the game they loved.

She wasn't sure whether to laugh or cry. Why did it all look so normal, so carefree and relaxed? Was no one going to rush out at some point and demand they all start behaving themselves? Ah, it suddenly made sense. There are other girls out in this world who are like me, she thought. Girls who love football. She felt a weight lifted from her shoulders as this realisation dawned on her. She wouldn't have to explain herself here.

Both the senior team and the Under-19 squad

were out on the pitch, A few of them looked over to greet her. She smiled back awkwardly. They seemed so cool, professional, so at ease with themselves.

And they spoke differently to her. She could feel her throat dry up as a couple of them attempted to start up a conversation with her. Negative thoughts started to tumble around in her mind:

'They'll laugh at how I talk, spot my northern accent straight away...'

Marta suddenly felt very alone again – the *'bicho do mato'* (or loner) she'd so often been called.

To distract her nerves, she started to warm up with stretches and exercises. She took a deep breath and thought of Tota, José Roberto, Valdemir and Luiz all back at home, probably all sitting down to watch a game together. They believed in her. Don't mess this up, Marta. You can't go back to Dois Riachos. Not yet.

Helena looked over at her and smiled. 'Just imagine it's any other game, Marta. Have fun.'

'Okay Marta, come on, pull yourself together,' she said to herself. 'What do you always do when you feel this way? That's right. Do what you always do. Express yourself on the pitch.'

The whistle blew and Marta's feet took over. She found herself sprinting, spinning and turning, with a pace and a power that immediately splintered the defence apart. As she got nearer to the goal she booted the ball with a kick so hard it sent the goalkeeper sprawling on her back when she tried to reach it. Marta watched as the ball rolled into the goal.

There was silence on the pitch for a while. Marta put her hands on her hips and turned around, unsure what to expect. She'd left a trail of defeated yet awe-struck defenders in her wake, all gobsmacked at the havoc she'd created in such a short space of time.

Heads continued to turn in her direction. People were staring. But not for the same reasons they stared at her back home. They were staring because they couldn't believe what they'd just seen.

Finally, she heard someone speak. It was Helena.

'We want her on our team.'

CHAPTER 14

"THE POWER IN THAT LEFT FOOT!"

It was a beautifully clear morning in Rio, and Marta could feel the breeze blowing in off the sea as she ran out onto Vasco da Gama's training ground, Estádio São Januário, with her teammates.

Marta had to pinch herself as they practised their finishing and crossing drills on large, plush green turf, so different to the scorched earth she was used to back home. She smiled as she thought of the small cubicle she'd changed into, compared to the facilities she shared with the girls now.

But what was more unbelievable was that she got to wake up to this, each and every morning.

As a member of the club she lived there too,

sharing a dorm with her teammates Ana and Nancey. She spoke to her mum once a week on the phone, for about five minutes, speaking nineteen to the dozen to get all her news in.

'You wouldn't believe it Mãe, the size of the building here – it looks so much bigger than it does on the telly.'

'We miss you Marta,' Mãe went on, 'but we're so glad you're happy there... just stay out of trouble and be a good girl.'

'They work me too hard here. I'm too tired to cause trouble!'

'You're still going to church, aren't you?'

'Yes, Mãe!'

'Are they feeding you properly?'

'Yes Mãe, I'm putting on some weight actually.'

Marta's skinny frame, that she'd felt so self-conscious about, was beginning to bulk out. She was in a training programme now, and there was a gym in the training ground. Her muscles were building each day, giving her even more pace and power on the pitch.

All the same, Marta missed her family desperately and thought about them as she closed her eyes each night. She thought about the boys in CSA and wondered if they missed playing with her. She smiled as she thought of the sun going down over the bridge, by the river she was told was too dangerous to play by.

Day by day, she felt her shy demeanour slipping. Here, no-one cared which part of the country anyone was from – they were just proud to be part of one of the biggest clubs in the country. Here they all belonged together, bonded through their love for the game, as they drilled and honed their techniques in the sun.

Marta also responded well to the sense of fun and spontaneity that was encouraged on the pitch. In between drills, some of the girls would show off and share their capoeira skills, playfully sparring with each other.

Others practised the miudinho – a type of samba dance, which Helena actively encouraged. As she explained: 'Domingos da Guia, one of the best players ever, adapted some of his moves from this.'

She added: 'The best Brazilian players swagger and sway – they use all of their body to make an impact on the pitch.'

Marta loved that she now had the space to explore and develop her own style, influenced by so many of the greats she admired from her own country's football legacy.

'I can place you anywhere on the pitch,' Helena told her in training. 'You have incredible speed, elegance and power. Plus you can score at will. But... you could still work on your passing.' She added: 'You're not a little child anymore.'

Marta hung her head a little at this in shame. She knew that she'd carved out the role of the loner for herself for a long time, perhaps almost without realising. She was so used to always being up against her opponents, never expecting to be helped out. Helena had a point – she needed to become more of a team player.

'If you focus on this,' said Helena, 'you've the potential to develop into an even more incredible striker. A wonder on the pitch.'

Now, thousands of miles away from her hometown, Marta was free to develop her skills. Sure, the women's team still got some giggles when they encountered the male teams but they all knew that they deserved their place there and that Helena was serious about building a game for women. Admittedly, there were still only two teams now, in one city, in the entire country, but it was a start. It was Helena's goal to have clubs all over the country for young women.

'And you girls will be a significant part of creating that.' She beamed at them. 'So no pressure – just play very, very well, better than the boys, okay?'

Marta felt very proud to be a part of this and it felt incredible to feel Helena's faith in them. She was still playing to prove herself, but this time someone wanted her to do well and not fail.

At Vasco's first home match against Flamengo, Marta couldn't wait to put the skills she'd been practising into action at her first senior professional match. They were playing to a very small crowd based entirely on the team's family, a tiny fraction of the crowd size that the men's team attracted but hey, it was still a crowd. She remembered Helena's advice. It was okay to want to be the best and strive towards that, but she needed her teammates too.

Within minutes of the whistle blowing, Marta took on the defence as she sped into the penalty area. Her heart swelled with joy as she heard the spectators gasp in surprise and amazement, while she segued her way through the defence, deftly moving the ball between her feet as though it was glued to her. But rather than always being on the attack Marta looked for new ways to use her pace to assist the strikers on the wings, switching from nifty passes with the back of her heel to longer shots that assisted a couple of goals in the first half.

There was plenty of team spirit, and when half-time arrived, as they ran back into the changing rooms, Marta finally and truly felt part of a team.

Energised by a brilliant first half, Marta focused in the second half on setting up opportunities for her teammates – but in the last twenty minutes she took a chance for herself. She was running down on the left flank as a defender came towards her anticipating a pass. Marta slowed right down before coming to a stop. She toyed with the defender for a few seconds, throwing in a few feints for fun, to show off her footwork. She barely looked at the goal mouth, as she slammed it into the top right of the net at an angle.

GOAL!!! Marta felt her teammates fall about her as she threw her head back and punched the air with her fists.

'Marta! Marta! That was amazing!'

As they ran off the pitch after the final whistle, Marta overheard people chatting excitedly about her:

'Did you see how she bent that ball around the defender?'

'The power in that left foot!'

'What pace – she never let them have the ball!'

Helena was beaming after the match. They'd conceded no goals and not given Flamengo any chances to break through the defence.

'Brilliant teamwork, girls!'

And it was that kind of brilliant teamwork that

Marta helped to develop further still: in 2001, when Vasco would go on to win the Brazilian Under-19 Championship, driven on by Marta's goals and determination.

CHAPTER 15

NATIONAL TEAM

As Helena ushered the team into the foyer of the stadium, Marta didn't feel good. She had seen that expression on Helena's face before. Something was up – what did it remind her of? Ah yes... her heart sank as she remembered her coach from CSA arriving on her doorstep that morning all of two years ago. She felt dizzy as alarming phrases tumbled from Helena's mouth:

'Girls.. I wanted you to hear from me... it's not been confirmed... but it looks as though we've just a few months left.'

The president of the club was axing the women's team. They hadn't been drawing the big crowds he'd hoped for, and so they were losing money. Of course it always came down to money, thought Marta. She'd been at Vasco over a year and, like her teammates, had completely dedicated her time and passion to the club.

Marta looked at the crestfallen faces around her. They'd all trained and played their hardest. But that commitment made no difference now – it hadn't counted for anything because they weren't drawing in enough money. There weren't enough spectators for women's football to keep it going. Marta realised this was one of their biggest obstacles – their fellow countrymen still had the mentality of the people she'd left back home. It wasn't just in Dois Riachos. It was in Rio, throughout the whole country, '*O País do Futebol*' (the country of football).

When it came to football, girls and women weren't taken seriously. As much as Helena assured them, they all felt as though they'd let her down. Marta had felt safe at the club. Perhaps too safe.

Many of her teammates were from Rio or the surrounding suburbs. Marta thought of the long three-hour journey back and the faces when she returned. She missed her family but Rio had been her home for the past year-and-a-half. She thought of her evening jogs by the beaches, the sunsets, kicking a ball back to kids along the shores and lilting rhythms of bossa nova at night. She thought of the money she'd been sending back to her mother to help her – it was a small monthly stipend but still, it was something that she knew made a difference.

'I can't go back now,' she thought. 'I just can't.'

*

Marta ran along the beach taking in the sights and smells of Rio waking up, which had become a regular part of her early morning exercise routine. Now that she was no longer training at Vasco she was determined not to let her fitness slip.

'Be prepared,' Helena said, 'you're not playing professionally right now... but that could all change.'

Helena was right – keep training as though you're about to play tomorrow. Her words had given Marta hope after the news of the women's team folding. She'd started playing futsal in one of the indoor clubs in the city at the weekends. It kept her playing and she enjoyed its emphasis on ball control and passing in small spaces, which helped her hone her techniques even more. She also received a small allowance from it, which she continued to send back to her family.

When she wasn't playing indoors she joined in with games down on Ipanema or Copacabana Beach. She loved to play barefoot, feeling the sand beneath her feet. She was living back at Marcos's family home, sleeping on the cot on the floor, but she was very grateful and ran daily errands for his wife whenever she could.

One afternoon, Marta arrived back at the flat to find that Helena had left a message to call her. Her heart skipped – she knew Helena was still exploring options for her. Perhaps there was news of another club who wanted to start a women's team?

'So Marta, can you cancel next month's session of futsal?'

'What?'

'I had an interesting chat with the Brazilian

Football Confederation. They want you on the national team, to play in Canada next month as a member of Brazil's Under-20 Women's World Cup team.'

Helena started to reel off some details. 'The money's not great... just a small monthly stipend, but...'

She started to laugh as she realised Marta wasn't even listening. The sound of her voice had long been drowned out by Marta's excited screams around the room. The Brazilian Football Confederation wanted her! She was to be a professional footballer playing for her country.

'They want me to double-check too... you're happy to play Number 10, I take it?'

Marta screamed even more with delight.

*

'Marta! Marta!'

At Vancouver's Swangard Stadium the crowd were cheering the name of the stand-out player, so far, from the 2002 Women's World Cup Under-19s tournament. As a team, Brazil were playing exceptionally, with forwards Cristiane and Kelly both consistently scoring terrific goals. But it was Marta's performance in their last game that everyone was talking about. She'd scored three of the goals in their 4–0 victory over France, ensuring they romped through to the quarter-finals, where they now faced Australia.

The accolades for Marta were pouring in:

'What bravado!'

'Such quiet confidence for one so young.'

'A joy to watch on the pitch.'

Marta was happy to receive the compliments, but she always remembered what her mother said about pride coming before a fall, and she retained her humility with the press after the match: 'The important thing is that we won. I was fortunate to score three goals.'

Marta had played well throughout and given a breakthrough performance but at the heart of it she was just overjoyed to be playing for her country. She still couldn't quite believe it as she stared down at her blue-and-green kit. Its bright colours had been worn by the heroes she'd watched on TV growing up, dancing and darting around, creating history. Now here she was, creating her own history.

It was early in the game but the chants of her name spurred Marta on. 'I'm here to score goals. I *want* to score goals,' she said under her breath. In midfield she picked up a long ball from Formiga on first touch. Within six seconds she'd raced down the field towards the goal, swivelling, spinning and swerving around each and every defender she came up against, in a solo run that finished with a smash from her famous left foot into the net.

GOAL!!! She heard the screams and shrieks of Cristiane and Kelly in her ears as the rest of the team leapt over to hug her. Marta made it two goals by the forty-fifth minute, but in the second half the Australian side fought back, pushing the game into extra time. However, Daniela saved the day in the hundredth minute and Brazil went through to meet Canada. In front of a 37,000-strong crowd at Edmonton Stadium, Brazil went out of the tournament on penalties, but their reputation as a formidable side was cemented.

After posing for photos, they took questions from an excited Canadian press.

'You've shown yourselves to be a great side with top players,' said one reporter. 'Do you think women's football will be taken more seriously now in Brazil?'

This was a tough question for them to answer.

'Whether it's taken seriously or not, we just want to concentrate on being the best that we can be,' replied Marta.

She added: 'Anyway, we think the yellow and green suits us better than the boys!'

CHAPTER 16

THE WORLD CUP

'Mãe! I've won the silver ball!' Marta garbled down the phone to her mother.

'The silver what?'

'Ball! It means I'm the second-highest scorer of the tournament!'

'Marta – that's wonderful news! I should never have doubted you – you had a dream and now you've succeeded. We wish we could watch it on TV here but...'

'I know Mum, I know, there's no way it would be televised.' Marta laughed at the thought. 'I don't suppose there's any news about me in Brazil, is there?' She heard silence on the other end of the line. 'Not even in Dois Riachos?'

'Well you know, Marta,' said Tereza. 'It takes a long time for anything to reach Dois Riachos. Including the rain! None for months here now... I've nearly used up the last of the water I collected.'

'Okay, well, I'll send you these newspaper clippings, mama...'

'Thank you, darling.'

'I think they'll want me on the senior team now – in next year's World Cup! It's in America this time! America! I can't wait.'

Luiz and José Roberto, who had come round to catch the phone call from Marta, were desperate to speak to her, especially when they heard this news.

'Marta! Do you know who else made their World Cup debut at the age of seventeen?'

'No – who?'

'Only Pelé!'

'Wow!'

'Pelé in a skirt! Pelé in a skirt!' they all sang in unison.

'Oh shut up!'

'Better get your bicycle kicks sorted, Marta!'

*

'Stop banging that cowbell, Cristiane – for goodness sake!' one of the girls in the dressing room cried.

'It helps me relax before a game – you know that!'

'Cristiane would have a whole samba band in here if she could!' laughed Marta.

'That's not a bad idea – I'm gonna ask Paulo if we can! Rosana – do you still have your carnival outfit? Let's all go out in make-up!'

'I thought we were trying to break down stereotypes here, girls!'

'Yeah, but it'd be fun! It's a carnival out there – can you hear?!'

Marta loved joking around with the girls like this before a game to help calm her nerves. This is what she would have loved as a kid, thought Marta, as she looked across at the broad and playful smiles of her teammates.

They were still a young and inexperienced team but Marta didn't feel this held them back. If anything, they played this to their advantage, springing about seizing opportunities with all the fearlessness of kids playing on the dirt tracks back home.

She felt an incredibly fierce bond with them as they walked out into RFK Stadium, in Washington, DC, to a crowd of nearly 16,000. They'd already beaten South Korea 3–0 in the group stages and survived their first test of nerves in the fourteenth minute with a penalty shot. Marta had stepped up to the task and coolly put it away into the net, taking away the 'Player of the Match' award at the end of it too.

But ultimately, Marta wanted to score goals. She hoped she now had her chance as the team faced Norway.

They knew Marianne Pettersen was one to watch – a towering experienced forward, who was one of their top scorers. In fact the majority of the team were far more experienced than they were. But within forty minutes both Daniela and Rosana had scored. On the stroke of half-time Pettersen reduced the deficit, but Brazil continued to hold their nerves in the second half.

In the fifty-ninth minute Marta saw a chance open up, when she picked out a rebound – from a shot by speedy midfielder Maycon – took a touch with her right foot, and drilled it past the defenders.

GOAL!!!

Kátia scored another six minutes later and a carnival atmosphere broke out in the stadium.

Brazil were through to the quarter-finals with Sweden.

*

'I'm afraid they just had a stronger defence.'

Brazil's coach Paulo tried to console the team. They'd lost to Sweden and were feeling incredibly sad and dejected, not least because they knew what it would have meant for women's football in Brazil.

'I wish I'd managed to block that first goal!' said Marta.

'We mustn't beat up ourselves up now,' said Paulo. 'We can only learn and grow from it. We're still a young team and have weaknesses we can improve on.'

Then he added: 'And Marta, again, another wonderful penalty. Thank you.'

As important as penalties were, Marta was getting fed up with being the go-to penalty girl. She could do it, but she was always happier scoring goals. However, she knew she'd played well in that tournament – she'd played many good balls and was always on the attack and taking chances.

During the tournament, Marta had been interviewed by a Swedish news station, which had described her as a 'young, promising player', alongside a feature they were doing on Brazilian forward Robinho, who played for Santos. Marta knew very little about Sweden but was happy the country was doing a segment on the women's game. As ever, she wished her own country would give her and the national team more coverage. They'd barely even covered this game.

She sighed as she started to think about the future. She was playing for Belo Horizonte back in Brazil, but there was still a feeling the rug could be pulled beneath her back home. There was always a fear that events were out of her hands – just as they had been the year before when she'd played for a small club in Minas Gerais. At the end of the season, the club had ceased its operations.

Little did she know that her life was about to change completely. But not in the way she was expecting.

CHAPTER 17

THE MOVE TO SWEDEN

'Hello? Is that Marta? I must say, you're hard to get hold of! Finally!'

Marta didn't recognise the voice on the phone but her suspicions were instantly raised, as the voice was speaking in Portuguese.

'Yes, I'm Odin Barbosa, and I work with the president of Umeå IK. I'm calling from Sweden.'

'Why would someone in Sweden be calling me? And talking in Portuguese?'

Her mind started racing. What did she know about Sweden? Yes, she'd played against them but there was too much of a language barrier. She knew it was up north somewhere. And it was cold. Very cold. People wore big woolly sweaters.

He went on.

'...We'd like to sign you to play for us...'

Marta snorted.

'José Roberto? Valdemir? Is that you?'

'No, no, it's Odin.'

'Mas que nada!'

She put the phone down. It rang back immediately.

'José Roberto – get out of here!'

It was no prank. The voice continued. 'I am Odin. From Umeå IK. And we want you.'

*

As the plane touched down in Stockholm, Marta wondered for the millionth time if she'd made a mistake in moving to Sweden. Her mum had prayed that God was sending her to all the right places, opening up all the right opportunities but why would he send her to this freezing cold country?

She put the Swedish phrasebook Odin had sent her for the journey to one side. She'd just about managed to master 'hej' and 'tack' for, respectively, 'hello' and 'thank you', but she could not imagine having a real conversation.

She wrapped the jumper her mother had knitted especially for her around her even tighter, and she looked out of the window at the dark hazy mist that surrounded the runway. It was early in the morning. Odin had warned her it would be particularly dark in the winter months but seriously, how did they even play football here? She already felt a pang for the beaches of Rio back home and the long summer nights of training by the sea.

Down the aisles, tall Amazonian-looking air hostesses prepared everyone for landing. Marta was used to feeling short but this was ridiculous. What if all the other players were this height?

She thought back to her conversation with Odin.

'What do you know about Sweden, Marta?'

'Er... it's very cold.'

'And?'

'ABBA?'

He laughed. 'Yes... so you don't know much more

than anyone else, then... Are you serious about football, Marta?'

'I don't think I would have got this far if I wasn't.'

'Indeed. Well, we're serious about it too. Crowds for the women's game here average around 900, far higher than in the rest of Europe. We also show club and international games live, to audiences of around 400,000.'

Marta thought of the state of play in her own country. No national league for women in Brazil. No interest from TV, newspapers or radio. Empty seats in the stadium and put-downs from the public who still held on to the steadfast belief that girls should be girls and boys should be boys.

Odin went on. 'You'd be playing for Damallsvenskan, the highest division of women's football in Sweden. You've got so much natural talent but I think this would be a great place for you to develop and have the chance to get even better. We're prepared to really invest in you if you work hard for us.'

He added: 'And you know what? I think you'll make us better too.'

Well, she hoped so, she thought, as she walked out onto the pitch of her new training ground at Umeå IK, Vännäsby, to meet her new teammates. She'd already made history. She was the first Brazilian woman to play professional football in Europe.

Yes, these women were all as tall as the air hostesses on the flight, if not taller. And quite serious looking too. At first glance, there appeared to be fewer broader smiles. Probably because they're all absolutely freezing, she thought... and no wonder. She felt her own face tensing up as a bitterly cold wind hit her. She saw a girl turn round to look at her, who she instantly recognised. It was Sofia Lundgren, the goalkeeper she'd scored a penalty against in Canada.

'Ah! It's you!' She waved and smiled. Then Sofia re-enacted Marta's penalty, pointing to her left boot and keeling over to one side as though she'd been knocked out. They both laughed. A few more players came over to introduce themselves, who Marta also recognised from the game – Anna Paulsson, Frida Östberg and Maria Bergqvist.

Maria said: 'Marta, we're on the same side now – be gentle with us!'

'Did you not bring the sun with you?' Frida joked. They spoke in bits of English or used sign language, and Marta attempted a few phrases in Swedish. Marta suddenly felt a lot more at ease. The weather may have been cold, but so far the people seemed warm and friendly.

'Anyway, you can't learn all the language at once,' she told herself. 'Just focus on the football'. As ever, her feet would have to do the talking.

CHAPTER 18

UMEA TRIUMPHS

'Hi Mãe!'

'Marta!' said her mother at the other end of the phone line. 'We've not heard from you in a while.'

'Don't worry, I'm okay, I've not been swallowed up by an avalanche – yet.'

'That's not funny, Marta.'

'I've just been busy. We train a lot harder here than back in Brazil.' Marta laughed and continued: 'I realise how lazy I was back home now. We're in the gym every day now. There is much more physical football here and the pace is higher. But it's good, I'm learning all the time.'

'Are you warm enough? Do I need to send more thermals? You sound exhausted.'

'Mãe, it's very cold but I'm getting used to it. And guess what? I went skiing the other day with some of the girls from the team!'

'That sounds dangerous, Marta, thank God we all pray for you every day.'

'It was great – I loved it! I wanted the snow to melt but I hope it stays now so we can go again.'

'Okay Marta... Well, please be careful.'

'I miss you all so much, Mãe.'

As well as the Swedish lifestyle, Marta was slowly adjusting her ear to the Swedish language. Its sounds were far more clipped and shorter than the long elongated vowels of her native language, which sounded more musical and rhythmic in comparison.

She was also adjusting to the Swedes' style of play. Although it was tighter, stricter, perhaps even a little more systematic than what she was used to, it was helping her to sharpen her technical skills. But in turn, she was influencing the team too.

With her moves, her flurries, her quirks, she was teaching them that they could only plan and rely on strategy so far, teaching them to give into the moment and trust that their feet, in fact the whole of their body, could do something brilliant, without them trying, pushing or forcing it. She was teaching them to improvise, to express themselves.

'It's okay to be you on the pitch, you know,' Marta laughed. 'No-one wants to see a bunch of robots all doing the same thing!'

It was the 2004 UEFA Cup Final. Marta ran out onto the pitch of Råsunda, and in its second leg, the pitch of the Stadion am Bornheimer Hang in Frankfurt, in her Number 10 shirt. The clear-cut lines of Umeå's black-and-white strip reminded her of the long wintry days ahead of her, in her new home. On either side of her were Maria and Anna – the other two forwards. As they lined up before play, the three of them danced a quick samba side step which Marta had taught them, exaggerating the movement of their hips. They all laughed.

'Remember to loosen up a bit, guys,' said Marta. 'Your power isn't just in your feet, it's in all of your body!'

Umeå had had a brilliant season. In the last few

games Marta had given some superb performances, scoring a hat trick when they beat Karlslunds 5–0. That was followed by four goals against Sunnanå, contributing to an 8–4 victory.

Now they faced Frankfurt, who they knew were a tough side, not least for the towering strength of their midfielder Birgit Prinz, a world class player, who was known for her wall-like defence. But as Marta so often found, Birgit could utilise her tiny frame to surprise taller defenders, who underestimated the devastation she could cause and reacted to her too late.

This was the case just before half-time. In the midfield Birgit hurtled through two defenders as they desperately tried to reach a ball pass. Marta picked it up and dribbled at speed towards the goalkeeper, nudging the ball to their left. In a desperate attempt to block the shot, the goalie fell to the ground – but not in enough time to derail Marta's determined right boot as she smashed it in to the top left of the goal.

Marta, Anna and Maria flew about the penalty dismantling the defence, with an instinctive feel for where each other were on the pitch. Between them they scored eight goals and conceded none, with Marta scoring her second hat trick of the season. They all lifted the cup high, but it was Marta who had been the star of the season.

When the game was over, there were young fans waiting outside the changing rooms desperately waiting for her to sign autographs. She was pleased to see a broad mix of boys and girls among the faces, calling:

'Marta! Marta!'

'Please!'

'Me! Me!'

Marta gasped in surprise as they shoved paper, pens and Umeå shirts in front of her. She'd never really thought about a signature before and wrote her full name.

Roland Arnqvist, Umeå's manager, laughed. 'You're just Marta now. That's what you're known as now.'

'This is so strange!'

'You'd better get used to it, Marta. You've scored twenty-two goals this league. You're a hero here!'

The accolades continued to flood in. The Swedish press were calling her the best football player in the world. A Swedish TV station, SVT, wanted to make a documentary about her journey from Brazil to Sweden.

Marika Domanski Lyfors thanked her personally. 'You've been a huge boost for the women's game here, Marta.' She added: 'And it's not just your playing... it's your smile, your spirit, your love for the game!'

Slowly, Sweden was beginning to feel like home. And Marta was proud of all that she had achieved there in such a short space of time. But there was a part of her that still felt torn – torn between her love for football and her love for her country. She missed the brightness and the warmth of their green-and-yellow shirts, the grins of her girls back in Brazil. She longed to play with them. Next year would be the Olympics in Athens. She hoped this would be her chance.

CHAPTER 19

MEDALS AND AWARDS

Pankritio Stadium, in Heraklion in Greece. It was late evening but the sunshine still beat down strongly on the exhausted Mexican players who, at 4–0 down, were losing to a still-energised Brazilian side.

Marta looked around the team with pride. There was Cristiane who'd scored twice in the match, and also Formiga, whose nickname ('the ant' in Portuguese) was one she'd picked up for her tireless work on the pitch. It had paid off twice in this match – once in the first half and then in the fifty-fourth minute. They were nearing the end now – clearly the victors, but it was always about scoring goals, wasn't it?

The crowd roared just a few minutes later, as Marta gained control of the ball on the left flank. Here we go, she thought, as she saw Mexico's beleaguered defenders attempt to run towards her. I can make this from here, she thought, as she slammed it at an angle through to the top right with her famous left boot.

GOAL!!! Marta leapt up and punched the air with her fists as Cristiane and Formiga joined her in line to do the samba swing in perfect time, as the crowd cheered.

The Brazilian team went on to lose against the USA in the final, but as they all collected their silver medals they knew that, even as a fresh, relatively inexperienced team they'd played incredibly well and proved to their country, if not the world, that they were worth watching.

Although it was difficult for Marta to leave her national team behind again, she was looking forward to seeing her Swedish teammates once more and starting a new season. Upon returning, she was also delighted to find out she'd been awarded the Goal of

the Year award at the 2004 Annual Football Gala in
Sweden. As she accepted the award, she grinned and
whispered to herself 'This will never get old for me!'

*

Two years later...

...And she was right! Marta had had a brilliant two
years on the pitch and, in the last few weeks of 2006,
Marta was nominated for Player of the Year at the
FIFA Awards for the third time. She hadn't won in
2004, or in 2005, but each time she was nominated it
felt even more surreal. In the grandeur and opulence
of Zürich Opera House she sat only feet away from
footballers she'd admired for years – Ronaldo,
Ronaldinho and Zidane. She knew her hero Rivaldo
had sat in this very room ten years ago. She looked
back on all she'd achieved over the past two years,
from her Golden Ball – awarded at the 2004 FIFA
Under-19 Women's World Championship – to her
great success in Sweden, the country that, for all its
contrasts to Brazil, was beginning to feel like home.

That evening, in that room, Marta was fully aware
she was part of a changing attitude towards women's

football. As she sat in her black evening gown she thought of the girl who'd fought to play in her oversized football top. Now, here she was – no more fighting, no more sense of shame, sharing an equal platform with some of the world's most respected players. 'I've shown them,' she thought, 'just by playing.'

She looked across at Kristine Lilly and Renate Lingor, the two outstanding world players she was up against. At the two previous FIFA Awards she'd come third, and then second, losing out against Birgit Prinz, the attacker she'd faced in Umeå IK's game against Frankfurt.

Marta's attention began to wander, and she thought of the conversation she had just had with her mother on the phone.

'You'll win this year!' Tereza had predicted on the phone. 'You'd better, Marta!'

Marta also heard José Roberto in the background, who called out, 'Don't let us down now!'

'If I win, mama, I'm coming home to celebrate. I promise.'

'You deserve to win, Marta.'

There was a pause before Tereza continued: 'I'm sorry I couldn't always give you the time, the time and support you deserved.'

Marta had welled up at this, and replied: 'I saw how hard you worked, Mãe, how tough you were. Where do you think I've got my strength from for all these years?'

And the winner... in first place... the FIFA Player of the Year is... Marta!!!

Marta's daydream was interrupted as she heard her name announced. Music started to play. Everyone was turning around to look at her expectantly. Marta's legs suddenly felt frozen to the spot as she felt a light tap on her arm from Odin sitting next to her.

'Go, Marta... go.'

Marta could see her shocked face magnified across a giant screen. 'Please don't cry now,' she thought to herself. 'Not yet – hold it in for a bit longer. Please no, not in front of Ronaldo.'

She managed to hold it together throughout her speech.

'I thank God for what I managed so far. My career has been a fantastic journey and I want to continue living this story for many years and keep learning from these amazing girls,' she said, turning to Lilly and Lingor.

After the ceremony she was inundated with questions from reporters. She had not realised she'd broken a record.

'You're twenty. How does it feel to be the youngest person to win?'

'Do you feel under pressure to keep achieving? What do you plan to do next?'

'I do not feel much pressure,' replied Marta. 'I just want to keep playing on my highest level.'

Suddenly, it all seemed clear to her. She'd worked so hard to be accepted, to carve out a place within the world of women's football. But this was only just beginning. She'd always wanted football to be fun. Amidst the desire to prove herself, she'd sometimes forgotten the simple joy of having a ball at her feet. And now it could be fun again. She had the whole world to play for.

CHAPTER 20

THE QUEEN OF FOOTBALL

As Marta boarded the bus back to Dois Riachos, the bus driver did a double take before breaking out into a huge smile.

'Ah – *La rainha do Futebo* – the Queen of Football!' He spoke in the strong northern Brazilian accent she loved and missed so much. 'My daughter loves you!'

Marta felt herself go bright red. The Football Federation had offered to fix her a car ride all the way home from Arapiraca Airport. But she wanted to take the bus. She didn't want to be alone; she wanted to immerse herself in the hustle and the bustle of the Alagoas people. The thought of rolling up in a car in front of her family would have been embarrassing, and they'd have brought her back down to earth quickly. She hadn't expected to be recognised, though.

'Please – will you sign this?' The driver found a beer mat, which she quickly scribbled on. As more and more people got on the bus, the more they recognised her. People grabbed their phones, asked for selfies as the vehicle rumbled through streets, stirring up the dust, along with old, long-forgotten memories.

Nothing could have prepared Marta for what she saw next, as they began their final descent towards the bus station she'd nervously stood at all those years ago. It was past midnight but she could hear noises off in the distance: samba drums thumping out the steady, yet offbeat rhythms she loved so well. Klaxons. Cowbells. Above it all, the sound of a berimbau cut through the din. What was going on? Was there a festival she'd forgotten about? Surely it was the wrong time of year for the Carnival of Brazil?

Then she saw the banners. The yellow-and-green shirts, a group of girls dancing and doing cartwheels in the streets. 'Marta'? Was that her name on one of the banners? 'Rainha do Futebol?' 'FIFA World Player?' Crowds. Crowds of people thronging the streets, all cheering as the bus pulled into the station. The driver couldn't get through. Everyone was shouting her name above the din.

In shock, Marta stumbled off the bus and found herself being lifted into a crowd of cheering, beaming faces. She recognised some of the faces. Some of them had even mocked and taunted her all those years ago. Now here they all were, laughing, waving and smiling. Finally, her family arrived in a fire truck, with her mum Tereza crying in the midst of it all.

In a daze, Marta was lifted onto the truck where she hugged and kissed her family, before the vehicle toured the streets of her childhood.

'How did you get this?' she laughed and cried, simultaneously.

'The town mayor said we could have anything!'

'I can't believe this! Why?? What??'

'They've all come to see you, Marta!'

'Marta – our hero is home!' Marta heard a voice she recognised from years ago through the din. It was Tota. He had aged a little, but he still had the same old kind eyes. He was clutching a pair of football boots in his hand that she recognised straight away. He held out a pen to her. 'Marta, would you do me the honour and sign these?' She took one look at him and burst into tears.

*

'I'm sorry but I need my feet! I can't leave them behind! But I'll leave my footprints behind, that's fine!'

Marta laughed as she pressed her feet into purple cement in front of the cameras, posing for photos and sticking her thumbs up. She had just made history. She was the first woman footballer to be inducted into the Maracanã's walk of fame, following her outstanding performance at the Pan American Games that summer. In front of a crowd of 68,000 at the Maracanã stadium in Rio de Janeiro, she'd helped lead Brazil to a gold medal win, in a 5–0 victory over the USA. Throughout the entire tournament she'd scored a total of twelve goals, wowing audiences across the world. Her feet now joined a long line of Brazilian legends – Romário, Garrincha, even Pelé. The indelible print she'd left on the sport was there for all to see, its significance undeniable.

Marta spoke for the cameras: 'This is important because it gives women an incentive to continue to fight for their space in all areas, and there's no doubt this has motivated each and every one of them to continue to fight, so that makes me happy.'

'What will your feet do next, Marta?' asked one reporter.

Everyone knew the answer:

'Play at the World Cup, of course!'

CHAPTER 21

CHINA 2007

'Nearly 50,000 out there!'

Brazil's coach Jorge Barcellos whooped as the Brazilian team huddled together in the changing rooms. They could hear the roar of the crowd outside in the Yellow Dragon Stadium in Hangzhou, China. It was the semi-final of the 2007 FIFA Women's World Cup.

Brazil's play had dazzled the world throughout the entire tournament, with Marta, Cristiane, Rosana and Daniela hailed as the 'fantastic four'. They'd glided their way through the group stage, defeating Australia in the quarter-finals. Now they faced the USA, a strong team, and Brazil knew they faced some tough defenders, including Stephanie Lopez and Kate Markgraf, as well as the legend Abby Wambach. But they felt as though little could defeat them now.

'Just keep doing what you're doing,' the coach continued. 'Make sure you push through on those chances to attack. We'll need as many as possible to withstand their strong defence.'

Jorge added: 'And Marta? We know you feel inferior about your size but try not to be intimidated by the height of Stephanie.' They all laughed. Marta was long over any insecurities about her size.

'But Hope Solo has made some incredible saves this tournament. We need to pull out all the swagger and sway that us Brazilians are known for!'

'Yeah!' they cried in unison. They couldn't wait to get out there and have fun.

'*Força Brasil!* Go Brazil!' the crowd chanted.

The roar of the crowd, as they ran out into the stadium, raised their spirits even more. They knew their audience was growing because of the work they were creating together – everyone wanted to see a piece of their Brazilian magic on the pitch.

Stations across the world were providing coverage
of the tournament including the BBC, and Brazilian
channels Rede Bandeirantes, SporTV, Premiere,
ESPN Brasil and BandSports. The tournament was
also being streamed live for the first time.

Marta was always overcome with emotion when
she stood and sang the Brazilian national anthem,
but the line 'Thou art a gentle mother, Beloved
homeland' had her choking back the tears. She
thought of all the team's mothers watching back
home, who'd probably doubted their children would
have the opportunity to end up doing what they
loved. Now here they all were, playing in a World
Cup semi-final with the world watching.

She thought of all her family, gathered around
the TV in Romero's bar, watching her game, just
as she had watched replays of her idol Rivaldo on
the same set, all those years ago. These moments
before the game were always a little like an out-of-
body experience to Marta – a few moments of calm
contemplation before they launched into the game.
Sometimes it surprised Marta how quickly they

could launch into the action of the game but they always did.

It started badly for the USA team. Within twenty minutes Formiga took a corner kick that hit the near post. The USA's midfielder Leslie Osborne tried to deflect it out but it went in, scoring an own goal. The Brazilian team were lifted by this early lead.

Seven minutes later Marta saw an opportunity open up, as she ran down on the right flank and into the penalty box with her usual tenacity. She quickened her pace, dodged one defender and left a trail of opponents in her wake, desperately trying to reach her in time. She didn't bother checking for Wambuch as she shot low and wide with steely determination, sending Briana Scurry the goalkeeper crashing to the floor.

GOAL!!

The USA team were unsettled and unable to break through the defence, while the Brazilian team kept on looking for chances to attack. In the fifty-fifth minute Formiga flew down on the left flank and passed to Cristiane. Ready and waiting to make it a third goal, she slammed it past the keeper.

The Brazilian fans and team were jubilant. They were nearing the end of the match with a 3–0 lead and knew they were securely through to the final. Marta felt them all relax. But why stop there? She wanted another goal. And she wanted to make this one great. That old familiar desire to win – not just for the team, but for herself – came rushing back.

It was the seventy-eighth minute. Marta picked up a long ball near the penalty box that she flicked over her left shoulder with her back left heel. She then wheeled right around her bewildered opponent, gathered the ball on the other side, and pirouetted around a second defender before pushing a shot with her right foot past the stunned goalkeeper. For a second she felt as though she was back on the dirt tracks again, simply playing, letting her body and feet fly and move whichever way they wanted. GOAL!!!

It had all happened so fast. She heard pure pandemonium echoing around the stadium. Her head swam as she felt Cristiane and the rest of the team fall all around her. Where had that come from? She had no idea but she knew it was special – perhaps the most special goal she'd ever scored. 'Thank you... thank you.' She crossed her heart and pointed to the sky as they danced their way to a victorious end.

The team jumped up and down excitedly in the changing room.

'Marta! Your goal – it's gone viral! Eleven million views!'

Marta was still in a daze. When she looked back online at that seven-second sequence she couldn't believe it herself.

'Pelé with a skirt!!!' The headlines went berserk the next day. Brazil had won but the world's eyes were on the team's Number 10 striker.

When she talked to the press, Marta remembered to remain humble.

'My goal is to be the best,' she said, 'and that is why I work so hard, but without my teammates I would be nothing.'

CHAPTER 22

LIVING IN AMERICA

In their hotel room, the girls all gathered around to watch the FIFA president Sepp Blatter speaking on the TV.

'Brazil have made incredible progress during this World Cup,' he said. 'But they've also achieved incredible progress for the women's game.'

The team whooped and cheered.

'Marta?' Jorge poked his head around the door. 'There's a call for you downstairs.'

Marta picked up the phone. 'Yes?'

'I hear they call you "Pelé with skirts..."'

Marta groaned. 'Yes... I'm kinda bored of that title already...'

There was a pause.

'Is this a journalist?' she asked.

'No. It's Pelé. I just wanted to say I'm honoured to have this comparison made.'

Marta's mouth dried up.

'This *has* to be a joke, right?'

'Congratulations on your win. I'm really enjoying watching the team. You're all brilliant.'

Marta dropped the phone and returned upstairs in a daze.

'Who was that?' Her teammates saw the look of shock on her face.

'Oh, you know, just Pelé... he just wanted to congratulate us on our win. He said he's really enjoying watching us.'

They all screamed the place down.

After the highs of that semi-final, the Brazilian team lost out to Germany in the final, unable to close down the towering defence of their top FIFA World player winner Birgit Prinz. Germany conceded no goals, an achievement they'd kept up throughout the whole tournament. Marta narrowly missed a penalty

– just tapping the goalpost, she then ran after the ball with her usual tenacity for a second attempt. But the defenders reached it in time.

Even though Brazil failed to win the World Cup, international viewing figures for women's football had soared and Brazil had provided extremely entertaining football that they were all proud of.

Furthermore, Marta had finished the tournament as the winner of both the 'Golden Ball', for top individual player, and of the 'Golden Boot' as the competition's top scorer, with seven goals.

*

The snow had just started to fall in Umeå. Marta smiled as she packed her new pair of flip flops, bikini and beach towel. She was looking forward to her next spell in the Californian sun. But more than that, she couldn't wait for the fresh challenge, a place where she could keep learning and honing her skills.

She'd just signed a three-year contract with Los Angeles Sol, as a Number 10 striker for the league's inaugural season. They shared the same ground as LA Galaxy where David Beckham played and were hoping to build on his new fanbase. Her Umeå team-mates gathered together glumly to say goodbye. Marta took a final look at her Number 10 shirt.

'Did you ever think you'd achieve so much wearing this?' asked Odin. After four consecutive seasons, Marta was leaving the club on an absolute high. They'd regained their title in the UEFA Cup, against Arsenal, thanks to Marta, who'd scored four goals. The game tasted like revenge. The previous season, Arsenal had beaten Umeå and won the title. The victory qualified the Swedish team for the semi-finals of the main European women's competition.

Odin continued: 'Of course, we will miss your amazing football skills – 111 goals in 103 games! But more than that, we'll miss the little bit of Brazil you've brought to this darker corner of the world.'

It had been a tough decision to make. After four years in Umeå she'd grown fond of their style of living and sweeping landscapes. She could even happily endure the tough winters. She was one of their highest-paid players now, and she continued to send money back to her mother that was helping her family to live a more comfortable life.

But since 1999, when the Women's World Cup had been held in the USA, the women's game was taken extremely seriously over there. The Women's Professional Soccer (WPS) League was attracting strong players from all over the world and Marta knew she'd be part of something special there. It felt right to go to America.

Tears welled up as she waved goodbye to her teammates. But she also had friends coming with her to Los Angeles Sol. Her friend and teammate Johanna Frisk was also joining the team as a defender. Cristiane was also moving to America to play for the Chicago Red Stars. Marta knew the move would have been harder for her without them.

It was great to feel the sun on herself as she ran with Johanna around the pitch, LA Sol's training ground. She looked all around at the beautiful mountains rising out of LA. They reminded her of Rio. She was happy to be back in her favourite Number 10 shirt too.

She'd already met some of her teammates before, playing against them in the 2007 World Cup. One of the team's defenders, Stephanie Cox, beamed at her: 'We're so happy to have you on the team Marta – it sure beats having you as an opponent!'

When Marta ran sprints over a series of hurdles, they all looked at her in amazement and almost burst out laughing.

'What? What?' asked Marta.

'You glide Marta... with total speed, it's kinda unreal to watch.'

She laughed.

'Unreal? The way you speak English is "unreal"... it's funny...'

Over the past four years Marta had become fairly fluent in Swedish. It was strange to revert to English again with her teammates and adjust to the American accent.

But as ever, their love of the game, and desire to connect on the pitch, overcame any language barriers.

CHAPTER 23

CALIFORNIA DREAMING

It was a clear bright day in May. Los Angeles Sol faced Sky Blue FC at their home ground.

New Jersey's Sky Blue FC had proved what a tough side they were since the start of the season, constantly strengthened by their experienced defensive midfielder Heather O'Reilly. Sol's defence was equally strong but they were nearing the end of the match and still hadn't broken through. Both sides were flagging and feeling the frustration.

Marta looked up into the crowds once more at the slew of 'I'm a Marta Maniac' banners. She smiled to herself. She loved to play but she was also spurred on by the thought of inspiring young players – 'the next generation', as their head coach Abner Rogers said. 'They're here to see you – the "Brazilian superstar",' as she was so often hailed in the press.

Marta also loved to see so many Latino and Brazilian families in the crowd supporting the game. Outside, fans had queued up for hours, desperate to get her autograph and be photographed with her.

'Come on, Marta,' she said to herself, 'do something. Don't let them down.'

In the eightieth minute, she picked up a long pass from midfield near the penalty box, realising she had a wide open space to play with. Sky Blue's defenders spotted this too late as they sped to catch up with her. But she'd already reached the penalty box. She dribbled at a furious pace towards the goalie as, in a valiant attempt to block her, they managed to kick the ball away, falling to the ground. Undeterred, Marta powered on, leaping over the legs of the sprawled keeper to reach the ball before slamming it low with her left foot into the goal.

GOAL!!!

Marta leapt up and down with euphoria as her

LA Sol teammates joined her to celebrate. As was so often her style, she'd saved the day in the final moments.

*

'Go, Marta!' The crowd whooped and cheered. Marta had just been awarded the Player of the Year trophy at the WPS Awards. The top goal scorer in the whole of the league, she'd totalled ten goals in nineteen appearances. In her acceptance speech, she said: 'I'm honoured to be a pioneer of the league. And everyone in this same room came in with the same objective this year – we all want to maintain the league for years to come.'

A few weeks later, Marta was to realise just how poignant these words were. After just one season, the WPS had decided to dissolve the team.

'This is so unfair, I know.' Abner Rogers hung her head in shame. 'But we don't have the cash to stay afloat.'

'I am a lady in waiting, yet again,' said Marta.

*

Marta's fifth FIFA win in 2011 felt bittersweet this

time round. Here she was, accepted for the fifth year in a row as the best female player on earth. After LA Sol had disbanded, she'd joined FC Gold Pride – also in California – before that folded, and then Western New York Flash. She'd taken both teams through to win the championship finals, finishing as top scorer in all three seasons. Yet WPS had cancelled the 2012 season and she found herself without a club or contract to her name.

Marta was used to uncertainty, but even with so many accolades and awards behind her, she yearned for some stability in her career. And, she laughed, she was still known as 'Pelé in a skirt'.

'Five times in a row,' she said through emotional tears. 'It's almost too good to be true.'

She paused. She suddenly realised she had an opportunity to share how she really felt. She owed it to the girls and women out there who loved football to tell the truth.

She went on: 'I dedicate this to my family but also to the struggle for women's soccer.'

Afterwards, the press probed her further. 'What

did you mean when you said "the struggle", Marta?'

'It's harder for women,' Marta explained. 'The men earn a lot of money, and they have a lot of clubs they can choose to play for. We work very hard, but we're always thinking about what might happen next year – if there's going to be a team or a place for us.'

'You sound stressed, Marta,' her mother Tereza said to her on the phone. 'It's not like you.'

'I don't know exactly where I'm going to go, that's why. It's tiring to keep changing from city to city every time. By February or March I should have a better idea.'

'I wish they had a national league here,' said Tereza. 'So you could come home and be closer to us.'

'I know, Mãe. But they don't. I'm afraid Brazil would still prefer it if we all stuck to samba dancing and beauty pageants!'

Her mother laughed. 'I'd like to see them try and force you into a bikini!' Then she said, 'Remember what you always said, Marta?'

'Show them on the pitch. Yes, but what if I don't even have a pitch to do that on, Mãe?'

A few weeks later Marta touched down in Sweden. She'd just signed to top tier league club Tyresö FF, based near Stockholm. She sighed as she saw the snow-capped mountains in the distance. She loved the States but it felt good to be back at her second home.

It was spring and she knew that much was expected of her in the next season. But as she saw the excited faces of her old friends Maria and Anna in the arrivals lounge, she thought to herself, 'Football can wait awhile – it's time to go skiing.'

CHAPTER 24

"FORÇA BRASIL!"

Marta looked up and gasped in amazement as fireworks exploded over the open rooftop of the Maracanã Stadium. She caught a glimpse of Cristo the Redentor, lit up in the green and yellow colours of the Brazilian flag, his arms outstretched across the city, as the opening ceremony of the 2016 Olympics carried on beneath him.

It was the first time a South American country had hosted the games and Marta was one of eight people chosen to carry the Olympic flag out in front of a stadium packed with 80,000 people. Marta felt honoured, but also terrified, to be sharing this incredible moment in history, with millions watching all over the world.

Her family had teased her about the flag:

'Hold on tight, Marta – don't drop it!'

'They chose you? Over Neymar?!'

Marta felt her hands sweat under the lights as she walked solemnly down the aisle dressed in a white suit, thankful that other star athletes were accompanying her in this task. When her name was announced she managed to smile and lift one hand to wave at the cheering crowd. It was a struggle to keep her composure but she knew she had a bigger task ahead of her.

With two silver medals behind them it was of course the Brazilian team's dream to win gold for their country, while hosting the games. Marta never took anything for granted and had worked and trained hard to make sure she was included in the team. At thirty years old, she was one of the oldest and more experienced players on the side, alongside her old allies Cristiane and Formiga, each with over one hundred caps to their names. Marta was aware that they would all be marked heavily because of this. But they also had younger, new players on their team – forward Andressa Alves and Raquel Fernandes.

'This mix will bring us good results!' declared their coach Vadão.

'Let's do this for Brazil. *And* women's football!' rallied Marta.

*

It was a baking hot evening at the Olympic Stadium, but the team knew they could cope in the heat as they sang their hearts out to the Brazilian anthem. They'd comfortably beaten China 3–0 in the last game and now faced Sweden, who they knew were tough opposition, with exciting and young new forwards that included Fridolina Rolfö and Stina Blackstenius.

It felt a little strange for Marta to be playing against Sweden – especially against her former teammate and friend Sofia Jakobsson – but she pushed it to the back of her mind.

'*Força Brasil!!!!*' '*Força Brasil!!!!*' With a crowd of

over 43,000, the team were determined to display the true spirit of '*joga bonita*' ('pretty play') that their country was known for.

But there was only one person Marta particularly cared about impressing tonight – her mother, who was sitting in the first few rows of the stadium.

As the whistle blew, the Brazilian team felt a lightness in their feet and a spring in their step, as carefree as the breeze that swayed above the shores off Ipanema Beach. In the twenty-first minute, a mix-up between the defenders let midfielder Beatriz sneak a goal into the empty net.

Three minutes after the first goal Marta found some space in the defence and assisted for Cristiane, who flicked it in to score a record fourteenth Olympic goal. The crowd were ecstatic as Brazil comfortably took the lead and the crowd couldn't get enough of it. In the forty-fourth minute Marta stepped up to take a penalty and didn't disappoint as she calmly belted it into the net.

But, oh, she longed to give the fans a goal. She persisted throughout, hot on the heels of Sweden's defenders. She heard the crowd chanting her name, desperate for their top player to perform some magic.

It was the eightieth minute. Marta could feel herself flagging a little but she picked up a pass from Beatriz, and accelerated towards the penalty box. The goalkeeper bravely attempted to block her in a one-on-one confrontation, but Marta never lost control of the ball. She shimmied around her at speed, her feet as light and adroit as they'd always been and slotted her second goal of the match home with her left foot.

GOAL!!! A carnival atmosphere broke out around the stadium. Marta fell to the ground punching the air as the team fell about her laughing and crying. 'Hang on! Hang on!' she cried as she ran towards her mum in the crowd, her arms outstretched with her hands cupped together to make a heart sign. Her mum was in tears, wiping her face with the Marta Number 10 shirt she was wearing.

Six minutes later Beatriz scored again, to make it 5–0, before Sweden grabbed a consolation goal back. As they left the stadium after the game they heard the chant: 'Marta is better than Neymar!' getting louder and louder. The team looked up into the crowds and saw a sea of T-shirts with Neymar's name scrubbed out on the back and 'Marta No 10' scrawled next to it in black marker pen with a huge heart.

The team stood still for a moment in shock at the sight of it, before breaking out into laughter. After the game they discovered that a young boy had started the T-shirt trend, after posting a picture that had gone viral. He had been frustrated that he couldn't get his own Marta T-shirt.

Marta now faced questions from the press.

'Marta, would you like to be thought of as the female version of Neymar?'

Despite the excitement of winning, Marta was as humble as ever. 'We have Marta, we have Neymar, we have Cristiane. We're all Brazilian.'

Brazil went on to defeat Australia, but heartbreak followed when they met Sweden again in the semifinal and were knocked out on penalty shoot-outs, finishing fourth in the tournament. Their dreams of gold were dashed but the whole team had felt a seismic shift in the level of support behind them.

Holding back tears at a press conference, Marta said:

'Our dreams may be dashed but what really matters to us is that we feel as though the whole country is with us this time. That's what really matters to us. The support has been incredible. They're really behind us and that's been the best feeling this entire Olympics. To be here playing in our country.'

CHAPTER 25

PRIDE

Marta shook her head in disbelief and clasped her hands to her heart as she walked through the arrival lounge of Orlando Airport. It was past ten at night and all she wanted to do was head straight for the hotel and get an early night ahead of the press conference.

She was not expecting the crowd of cheering fans who'd congregated to welcome her, waving Orlando Pride banners and Brazilian flags. Marta's face broke out into the huge infectious smile her fans had grown to love as much as her football playing, as she began signing footballs and the purple Orlando Pride kit.

'Wow,' she thought, 'if the fans are always this supportive, I can't wait to get started!'

She'd recently signed to the Orlando team, who were a part of the National Women's Soccer League (NWSL) – the top professional women's soccer league in the USA.

Marta spotted a small girl of about six staring up at her. She was clinging shyly to her mother's legs. Her mother spoke: 'She's just started playing football and you're her absolute hero. She wants to know how she can get to be where you are.'

Marta bent down and smiled. She thought of herself again at that age. There had been no role models, no one to follow or tell her the steps to take. She had just followed a long line of Brazilian footballing heroes, darting about joyously on a screen in her hometown, giving her hope that she too, one day, might have a pitch to play on, as crazy an idea as everyone else around her believed it to be.

'Do you love playing football?' Marta asked the girl.

'Yes.'

'Never forget that. Because you'll hear the word "no" a lot. "No, you can't do it", "No, you're not good enough", "No, you should give up." But if you love and believe in what you do, the nos won't matter, you'll just keep going. Do you promise me to trust and believe in yourself?'

The girl nodded.

Marta realised that in the past few years, there had been a shift in what she wanted to achieve. Yes, she wanted her career to keep going for as long as possible, she wanted to have a successful season for Orlando Pride and ultimately score goals. And of course she, along with the Brazilian national team, still dreamt of feeling the weight of gold in their hands – achieving the Olympic dream for their country. The year 2020... it was still possible.

But her priorities were changing. She had become empowered through playing football. It had changed her life completely and given her the chance to help her family, meet other people, see other countries and experience other cultures. Life was no longer just about her or the team's individual goals anymore.

It was about giving back. It was about representing all the girls across the world, who wanted to play football. It was about doing justice for all those young women who had felt like her at some point – isolated, different, alone.

And she knew just how important that still was in her home country. As part of the Olympics legacy of 2016, and in her new role as a United Nations Goodwill Ambassador, she worked with young women and girls in Rio de Janeiro to provide sport and life-skills training. One day, she wanted to return to Dois Riachos and see girls playing football with boys in the streets, on the fields, in the tournaments, for it to be 'normal', for there to be no weird stares or mean comments.

Marta knew that there was still a long way to go until that became a reality for all girls everywhere, all over the world. But, as with all the journeys that had taken her to the top, she was prepared to take it one step at a time.

MARTA
HONOURS

Umeå IK
🏆 UEFA Women's Cup: 2003–04

FC Gold Pride
🏆 WPS Championship: 2010

Western New York Flash
🏆 WPS Championship: 2011

National team
🏆 Pan American Games: 2003, 2007
🏆 Sudamericano Femenino: 2003, 2010, 2018
🏆 FIFA Women's World Cup: 2007 – Runner-Up

🏆 Silver medal at the Summer Olympics: 2004
and 2008

Individual

🏆 FIFA World Player of the Year: 2006, 2007,
2008, 2009, 2010

🏆 The Best FIFA Women's Player: 2018

🏆 FIFA Women's World Cup Golden Ball: 2007

🏆 Women's Professional Soccer Golden Boot:
2009, 2010, 2011

🏆 IFFHS World's Best Woman Playmaker: 2012

🏆 IFFHS Women's World Team: 2018

🏆 Copa Libertadores de Fútbol Femenino Golden
Ball: 2009

🏆 Damallsvenskan Top Scorer: 2004, 2005,
2008

MARTA

10 THE FACTS

NAME: Marta Vieira da Silva

DATE OF BIRTH: 19 February 1986

AGE: 33

PLACE OF BIRTH: Dois Riachos, Alagoas, Brazil

NATIONALITY: Brazilian

POSITION: Forward

THE STATS

Height (cm):	162
Club appearances:	362
Club goals:	276
International appearances:	133
International goals:	110
International trophies:	5

★ ★ ★ **HERO RATING: 94** ★ ★ ★

GREATEST MOMENTS

Type and search the web links to see the magic for yourself!

★ 1

27 SEPTEMBER 2007 FIFA WOMEN'S WORLD CUP BRAZIL 4-0 US

https://www.youtube.com/watch?v=UZywdRNArnw

Marta scores the fourth goal of the match in this crucial semi-final match against the US. The footage went viral and astonished audiences all over the world. Marta still describes it as 'the most beautiful goal I've ever scored'.

2 3 JULY 2011 FIFA WOMEN'S WORLD CUP BRAZIL 3-0 NORWAY

https://www.youtube.com/watch?v=TS2Ezvteyqk
After a controversial first goal in the twenty-fourth
minute, Marta steams through Norwegian defenders
in the second half to provide an assist for teammate
Rosana. She then slams in a shot two minutes later,
to make the final score 3–0.

3 9 JUNE 2015 FIFA WOMEN'S WORLD CUP BRAZIL 2-0 SOUTH KOREA

https://www.youtube.com/watch?v=sLhfyZmridI
This is a historic match for Brazil as Marta becomes
the all-time World Cup leading scorer, converting a
penalty kick in a 2–0 win over South Korea.

7 JULY 2018 ORLANDO PRIDE
2-1 WASHINGTON SPIRIT

4

https://www.youtube.com/watch?v=HETdntktLYI

In the eighty-sixth minute Marta scored the winning
goal for Orlando Pride. It also tied her with Alex
Morgan's record for most goals in club history (16).

PLAY LIKE YOUR HEROES

THE MARTA DRIBBLE

SEE IT HERE You Tube

HTTPS://WWW.YOUTUBE.COM/WATCH?V=RHISNTX3JYY

STEP 1: Run directly at a defender, backing them into their own box. Be fearless!

STEP 2: Throw in a couple of quick stepovers, circling first one foot around the ball, then the other. They won't know which way you're going.

STEP 3: Cut inside, towards the centre of the pitch, as suddenly as you can. Now they're off-balance, and you're closer to goal.

STEP 4: Don't slow down now! If the defender has kept up, now's the time to fool them with a little 'Cruyff Turn', to create space for a shot. Shape as if to shoot, but use the inside of your foot to suddenly drag the ball back behind you instead. Now you've lost them!

STEP 5: You're through on goal. So stay calm, fool the keeper with your eyes and slot coolly past them into the bottom corner. Clinical!

TEST YOUR KNOWLEDGE

1. Which Brazilian football hero did Marta look up to at school?

2. What materials did Marta make footballs from?

3. What was the name of Marta's first coach?

4. What does fome de bola mean?

5. What was the name of the famous Maceió football club that wanted to pick Marta?

6. What was the name of Vasco de Gama's training ground?

7. What number shirt did Marta wear when she joined the Under-20 Women's World Cup team?

8. In what minute did Marta score against Norway in the Under-20 Women's World Cup team?

9. What's the name of the team that Marta plays for in Sweden?

10. What medal did Brazil take home in the Athens Olympics, 2004?

11. Which other two female players was Marta up against for FIFA Player of the Year in 2006?

12. Marta was the first female footballer to be inducted into the walk of fame at which stadium?

13. Which players were hailed as the 'fantastic four' in the 2007 FIFA Women's World Cup?

1. *Rivaldo* 2. *Paper, cloth and plastic bags* 3. *Tota* 4. *Ball hunger*
5. *Centro Sportivo Alagoano (the youth system)* 6. *Estádio São Januário*
7. *Number 10* 8. *59th* 9. *Umeå IK* 10. *Silver* 11. *Kristine Lilly and Renate Lingor* 12. *Maracana* 13. *Marta, Cristiane, Rosana and Daniela* 14. *Orlando Pride*

Answers below. . . No cheating!

14. Which NWSL team did Marta sign with on her return to the USA in 2016?

CHARLOTTE BROWNE

HAVE YOU GOT THEM ALL?

This summer, the world's best footballers will pull on their country's colours to go head to head for the ultimate prize – the FIFA Women's World Cup.

Celebrate by making sure you read the stories of three more Ultimate Football Heroes!